MICH   7975
977.40' May WIT

Pictorial History of Michigan:
The Early Years

DATE DUE

FE 17'73	JUN 2 '82	DE 13 '91	
JY 2'73	AG 13'8	JY 9'93	
MY 4'7	FE 28 '83	AG 24'95	
JY 27'74	AP 30 '83	MY 17'96	
MR 21'7	DE 22'8	JY 1'9	
MY 17'75	AP 27'8	SE 18 '98	
MR 10'7	SE 24'8		
JY 3 '7	JA 3 '8	E 7 00	
E 6 '77	DE 16'8		
MY 19'78	DE 15'9	JA 05 '0	
MR 27'8	MR 09'9		
	JE 15 '91		

PICTORIAL HISTORY
OF MICHIGAN:

The Early Years

PICTORIAL HISTORY OF MICHIGAN:

The Early Years

by

GEORGE S. MAY

Associate Professor of History
Eastern Michigan University

A John M. Munson Michigan History Fund Publication

MICHIGAN HISTORICAL COMMISSION

DEPARTMENT OF STATE

WILLIAM B. EERDMANS PUBLISHING COMPANY
GRAND RAPIDS, MICHIGAN

CONTENTS

FOREWORD

"I consider it important that the citizens of Michigan have adequate and correct knowledge of the history and functions of the state of Michigan and its institutions and that this should be taught to the young people in its schools and colleges." This was the judgment of Dr. John M. Munson when he established a trust fund for the publication of works dealing with Michigan history. A native of Pennsylvania and a graduate of Michigan State Normal College, Dr. Munson devoted his entire career to Michigan education. He served for a number of years in the State Department of Public Instruction, spent ten years as president of Northern State Teachers College (Marquette), and for a decade and a half was president of Michigan State Normal College (Ypsilanti). With a lifelong interest in the history of his adopted state, he established the John M. Munson Michigan History Fund and entrusted the Michigan Historical Commission with responsibility for the publication of such historical material.

The first book-length publication of the John M. Munson Michigan History Fund, F. Clever Bald's *Michigan in Four Centuries,* appeared in 1954 and almost immediately became the standard textbook treatment of Michigan history. Because of enthusiastic public response, the Michigan Historical Commission began the next year to gather material for a pictorial history that would serve as a companion volume to this scholarly book. The Commission Archivist, Dr. Philip Mason, now head of the Labor History Archives at Wayne State University, was the first director of the project, which was later carried through to completion by another staff member, Dr. George S. May. Early in 1966, Dr. May joined the staff of Eastern Michigan University, but he continued to work on the pictorial history. This volume is mainly the result of his dedicated efforts. His many other publications in the field of Michigan history, particularly those on Mackinac and the Civil War and his articles and reviews in regional historical quarterlies, give ample evidence of Dr. May's competence in this field.

The result of a dozen years of work by the Michigan Historical Commission, the *Pictorial History of Michigan: The Early Years* has been compiled with the hope of bringing to Michigan citizens a broader knowledge of the rich heritage of this region.

Hudson Mead, President 1966-67
Michigan Historical Commission

INTRODUCTION

In the world of the Twentieth Century, Michigan is generally distinguished from the other forty-nine members of the United States of America by its unique geographical outlines and by the fact of its association with the automobile industry and, to a secondary degree, with other manufacturing activities.

This has not always been the case. Although Michigan's geographical features have remained the same as long as mankind can remember, the products for which Michigan has been famous have changed greatly through the centuries. Before Michigan was a state, long before there was a United States, Michigan was known for its furs. Later, it became renowned for the fish that were found in the waters that separated its two great peninsulas, for the pine and other timber found in the vast forests that covered these peninsulas, for the rich soils that were found to the south, and for the equally rich mineral deposits in the northern reaches of the state.

For nearly three hundred years after Michigan first appears in the recorded annals of history, this area was part of the American West, a land of opportunity for anyone, be he fur trader, fisherman, lumberjack, miner, or farmer, who had the courage and the strength to wrest from this land the wealth nature had bestowed upon it. This book is an attempt to recreate, through pictures, that earlier Michigan which preceded the modern Michigan of the automobile and the freeway, the urbanized and industrialized state in America's Middle West which is famous, not for its natural resources, but for the products of its factories and laboratories.

The very term pictorial history is, to some extent, a misnomer, since any historical account must be based primarily on written records and no amount of pictures can provide the detailed knowledge and understanding that such documents provide. Yet historians who neglect the pictorial records do so at their own risk. One picture may or may not equal a thousand words, but the insight into the individuals who made history and into the conditions under which they lived that can be gained through a study of the pictures from a particular era is something that cannot be measured.

In an effort to approach the view of this earlier era in Michigan's history that was held by those who lived it, I have confined my selection, with only a very few exceptions, to illustrative material from the period or to photographs of physical objects that existed in those years. This means that the kind of re-creation of historical events by artists of a later generation that the reader may be accustomed to seeing in pictorial histories will not be found here. Although there are many paintings of this type that relate to topics included in this book and although their use would add considerable color, they have been excluded in the interests of historical authenticity. It is hoped that whatever may have been lost by this omission will be more than made up by the unusual variety of illustrative items of an original, historical character which I have been fortunate enough to locate and include in the pages that follow.

In any history, the historian must select the material he includes. This selectivity is probably most evident in a pictorial history. Many who are familiar with Michigan history will no doubt find that some of their favorite pictures have not been included or will think that certain topics deserve more attention than I have given to them. Space limitations, plus a desire to reproduce the pictures on as large a scale as possible, made it necessary to exclude much good material and to slight or leave out entirely some subjects. The decision as to what to include was made on the basis of my own personal, no doubt subjective, view of what was important as far as the present book is concerned.

In a work of this nature, many people and many organizations and institutions are involved. Elsewhere in the book I acknowledge the debt I owe to all those who aided in the collection of pictures. In addition, however, I should like to express my appreciation to several others without whose help and co-operation this history would never have been completed. I began this book when I was research archivist with the Michigan Historical Commission but I did the bulk of the work after joining the faculty of Eastern Michigan University. At all times the Commission staff was generous in its assistance while the expenses attending the collection and reproduction of pictures for the book were underwritten by the Commission's John M. Munson Michigan History Fund. To William B. Eerdmans, Jr., the publisher, is due the credit for suggesting the project in the first place and for his never-flagging desire to see that the physical appearance of the publication would be of the finest quality possible. Working with him and his staff, particularly Cornelius ("Casey") Lambregtse, who is responsible for the splendid design and layout of the book, was for me one of the most pleasant features of the entire project.

Finally, I am grateful for the support and encouragement of my wife during what must have seemed to her the interminable period that I worked on this book.

GEORGE S. MAY

Ann Arbor, Michigan

12

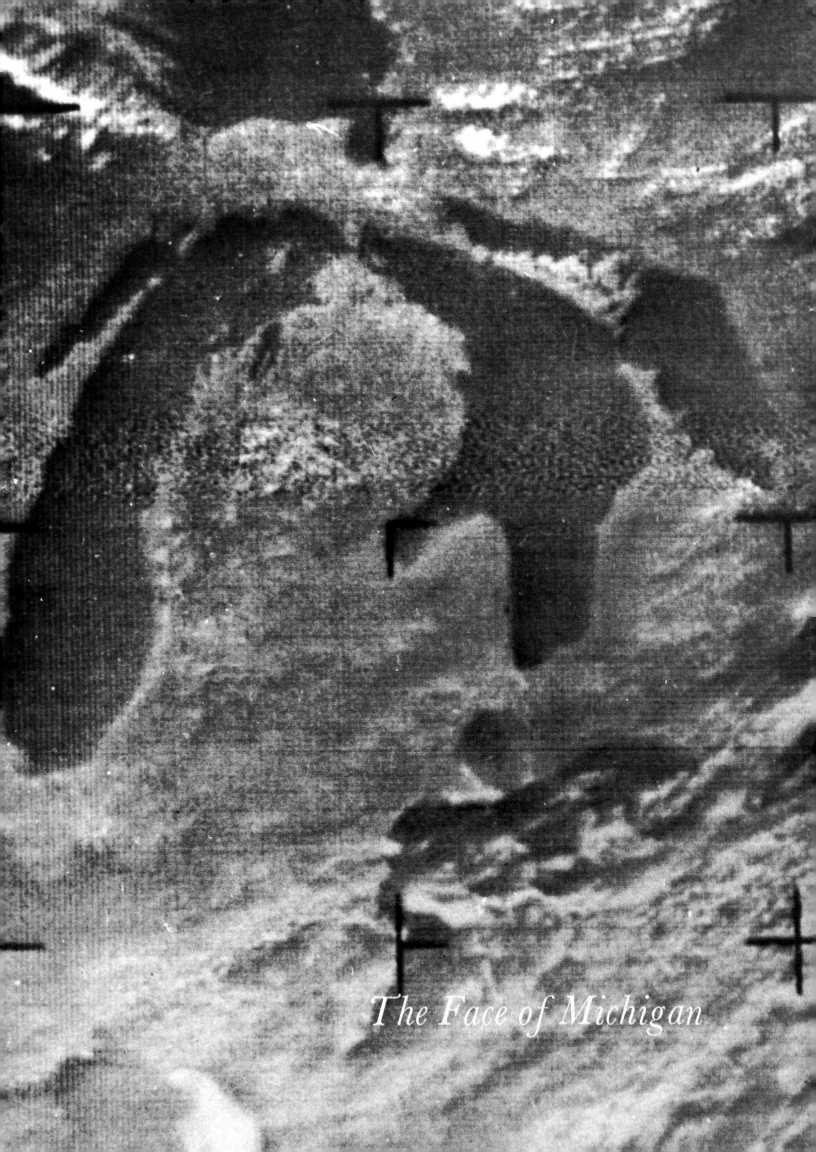

The Face of Michigan

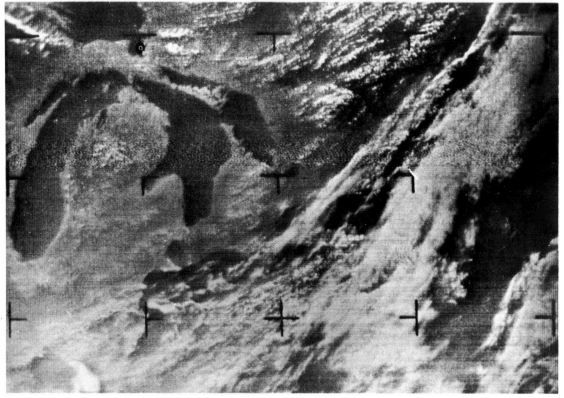

There could be no doubt about it. Through the clouds that obscured some areas to the east, the camera of NASA's weather satellite, Nimbus 1, had photographed the upper Great Lakes and the peninsulas that divide these vast bodies of fresh water. Even from five hundred miles above the earth's surface, the familiar outlines were clearly visible. The date was August 29, 1964. Michigan had had its picture taken.

Courtesy: Wide World Photos

Three centuries before the camera of Nimbus 1 recorded Michigan's image, the future state's distinctive geographical features were being gradually revealed to the civilized world of western Europe. The French, who had begun exploring the St. Lawrence River valley in the sixteenth century, probed ever deeper into the continent in the early decades of the 1600's. The extent of the knowledge which they gained was indicated by the French royal cartographer, Nicolas Sanson d'Abbeville, in this map of Canada or New France, published in 1656. All five Great Lakes are shown, although Sanson left Lake Superior and Lac de Puans (Lake Michigan) open-ended on the west, candidly admitting his ignorance of these interior regions. Although the shape of Michigan's two peninsulas was beginning to emerge on this map, Michigan as a geographical and political unit did not then exist, nor would it for another century and a half.

Courtesy: William L. Clements Library

The land which the French found and which is now called Michigan was then, as much of it still is today, a vast wilderness, covered with magnificent stands of timber, such as can be seen in Hartwick Pines State Park near Roscommon, timber that would later prove a source of seemingly unlimited wealth.

Courtesy: Michigan Department of Conservation

Although the green foliage that covered their surfaces imparted to Michigan's two peninsulas a certain sameness in appearance, the French soon discovered that there was actually a surprising variety in the topography of the area. There was a rugged character to the northern, or Upper Peninsula, as, for example, in the Porcupine Mountains in the west . . .

15

. . . or in its many waterfalls, especially the most majestic of them all, Tahquamenon Falls, near the peninsula's eastern end . . .

. . . or in such spectacular phenomena as Miner's Castle, part of the Pictured Rocks, which, for all their beauty, are dwarfed by the cold majesty of Lake Superior, the world's largest non-saline lake, whose waters wash the entire northern shore of the Upper Peninsula, adding a certain harsh, yet appealing, feature to the peninsula's character.

16

A characteristic of lower Michigan is the rivers which flow to the east or to the west from a watershed running up through the center of the peninsula. Near the northern tip, a tortuous network of connecting lakes and rivers forms an inland waterway running from Lake Huron almost all the way across to Lake Michigan.

In the central part of the lower peninsula, Dead Stream Swamp, northwest of Houghton Lake, provides still another element of variety to Michigan's landscape. The Muskegon River, at the lower left, joins the Dead Stream, lower right, and the waterway then snakes its way down toward Reedsburg Dam.

17

On the lower peninsula's western shore, the prevailing winds sweeping in from Lake Michigan have brought about the formation of huge sand dunes such as this one, the giant, Sleeping Bear Dune. The winds, the lake, and the sands combined to provide the basis for a prosperous recreation industry and a climate that would foster the development of a bountiful fruit-growing agricultural economy.

Courtesy: Michigan Tourist Council

Northern Michigan's topography, the French found, contained much that was spectacular and strikingly beautiful, but it was the gently rolling, fertile lands of the southern third of the lower peninsula that would become home for the vast majority of the millions of people who came to reside in Michigan in the centuries after the French arrived. This characteristic of the terrain of southern Michigan also made the task of the twentieth-century road builder easier. This view is of the area around the I-96, US-27, and M-78 interchange, south of Lansing.

Courtesy: Michigan State Highway Department

The Prehistoric Indians

The French were not the first people in Michigan, for when they began arriving in the 1600's they were greeted by several thousand Indians, such as the Ottawas, one of whom was sketched by a Frenchman of somewhat primitive artistic talents.

The untrained eye sees little evidence of Indian life at the Spring Creek site, and, in fact, pitifully few remains are left of the people who inhabited Michigan for possibly ten thousand years before the first white inhabitants arrived. The best-known visible remains have been the mounds which these prehistoric Michiganians built for burial purposes and perhaps for other uses. The largest reported in Michigan was the great mound on the River Rouge, a half-mile from the Detroit River. It was seven to eight hundred feet long, four hundred feet wide, and at least forty feet high when viewed by Americans in the early nineteenth century. By the 1880's, when this sketch was published, it had been reduced to half its original size, and since that time it has been completely leveled.

Michigan's Indians, whose sole means of transportation was the canoe, were scattered over the two peninsulas, camping principally along the numerous waterways. One such campsite, located on high ground overlooking Spring Creek in Muskegon County, has been excavated by archaeologists, who determined that the site was occupied sometime around A.D. 1000.

Courtesy: Grand Rapids Press

The largest surviving group of authentic Indian mounds in Michigan are these, known as the Norton Mounds, located near the Grand River, west of Grand Rapids. They date from the time of Christ. The gravel pit in the foreground, dating from 1963, is a symbol of the forces of progress which erase the past in the name of the present.

Some of the Norton Mounds were excavated in 1963-64 by the University of Michigan and the Grand Rapids Public Museum. The archaeologists carefully dug down through the topsoil and into the mound itself, finally reaching the level at which bodies had been buried in a period in world history when France and England were mere outposts of the Roman Empire.

The skeletal remains found in one of the Norton Mounds are shown here, together with artifacts that were buried with these Indians.

Courtesy: University of Michigan Museum of Anthropology

Courtesy: University of Michigan Museum of Anthropology

21

Through a study of pottery, bone implements, and other artifacts found in the Norton Mounds, and by comparing them with artifacts found elsewhere, archaeologists are gradually able to piece together a picture of the cultural development of the prehistoric Indians.

Courtesy: University of Michigan Museum of Anthropology

Long since obliterated by the white man's plow are the so-called Garden Beds which nineteenth-century settlers found in Kalamazoo County and a few other areas in the state. The exact purpose, whether ceremonial or utilitarian, that these ridges of earth, carefully laid out in geometric patterns, in some cases covering five acres, were intended to serve is a disputed subject. These, which were found in Kalamazoo County, are outlined in *Memorials of a Half-Century,* by Bela Hubbard, who declared that they were the most common type found by the pioneers. By the 1880's, when he wrote his book, however, Hubbard was unable to find scarcely a trace of any of the Garden Beds.

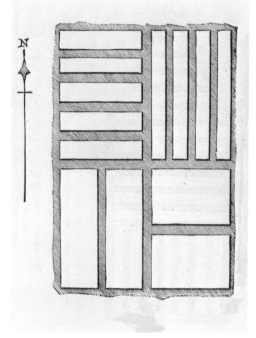

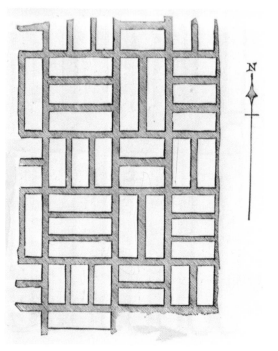

Indian rock carvings and paintings, which have furnished clues to the life of the prehistoric Indians elsewhere in the New World, are almost nonexistent in Michigan. One exception are the carvings on rock outcroppings near the confluence of the north and south forks of the Cass River in Sanilac County.

Time's weathering action has nearly erased these Sanilac Petroglyphs, as the engravings are called, but they are still visible, especially when the incisions are traced with chalk. What special meaning, if any, this figure and the geometric design held for the Indians who made the carvings can only be guessed.

Closely related in design to the Sanilac Petroglyphs are paintings, presumably of Indian origin, high above the water line of sheer rock cliffs known as Burnt Bluff, near Fayette on the southern shore of the Upper Peninsula.

But the best-known relics of Michigan's prehistoric Indians are the arrowheads and other stone implements which the farmer's plow and the amateur archaeologist's shovel have turned up by the thousands all over the state. Unless each such artifact is carefully identified as to where it was found, it is of little use to the anthropologist or professional archaeologist. Nevertheless, these simple, man-made weapons and tools can assist their finder in conjuring up a picture of the individuals who manufactured them, and who lived and died in Michigan over a period of years many times longer than the length of time that today's non-Indian inhabitants and their ancestors have resided in the same area.

The Age of the French

Ce Canton est entièr

SUPÉRIEUR

Isle Maurepas

I. Pontchartrain

I. Hoquart

I. St. Anne

I. Beauharnois

Isles S. Ignace

eaux Minong

Srouagache

Isle du Pic

Test de l'outre

Baye de Michipicoton

Cap des Chaillons

Ance aux Sables

Minabaujou

Cap Hoquart

R. Rouge

R. aux Testes bould

Havre de Beauharnois

R. de Beauharnois

R. à Charon

R. au Galop

Mamens

Baye de Bachouanan

R. Bachouanan

Pointe aux Chenes

Ance à la Poche

Gros Cap Sault Ste. Marie

Mission St. Marie

Pointe aux Tessalons

LES SAUTEURS

Toute cette Coste n'est point

R. du Luth

R. Torne

R. des Saute

Isle Manitoualin

Les Amicoues Habitent cette Isle

LAC HURON

les Pays plato

Village d'Outouaco

R. de Belle chasse

R. des Hurons

Village de Mississagués

Lac de St. Claire

Neutre Detroit

Village d'Outouaks

R. du Detroit

R. des Cedres

Petit Etang

les Petits Ecores

Le Detroit

la Pointe Pelée

I. des Serpens Sonnettes

P. de S. François Xavier

Ance de Quouicouan de la Roche

Niamicou

la Grande Isle

le Portail les Grands Sables

I. aux Erable

aux S. Princesses

R. aux Cheeru

R. au Parcsvaux

R. de la Mauvaise

R. Hicamerque

le Grand marais

Pointe au Poisson Blanc

F. et Mission détruite

Machillimakinac

I. Ste. Helène

I. aux Bois Blancs

Mission le Fort S. Ignace

Ance au Tonere

Deux Rivieres dont on ne connoit pas le Cours

B. des Noquets

I. du Castor

l'Ours qui dort

Grande Traverse

R. aux Buscies

R. d'Oulamanitu

R. du P. Marquet

R. S. Nicolas

R. aux Sables

R. Blanche

R. Mastcon

la Grande Riviere

R. au Raisin

R. à la Barbue

R. Macamea

Riv. Noire

Terrain plus

B. de Saguinam

Portage

Elavé

I. des Pouteoutamis

Village des Malomines

R. des Puans

le Fort les Otchagres

Les Sakis

Mission de St. François Xavier

LAC

MICHIGAN

R. et Fort de Chicagou

R. Galline

Portage aux chénes

Village de Miamis

Village de Poutouatamis

le Fort Portage

Sourceda Teakiki

R. S. Joseph

R. des Miamis

Sources de la Riv Ouabache

Portage

Toute cette cost

Perrage

des Renards

Depost

a Marine

levoix.

graphe

R. des Ilinois

la Fourche

Riviere de Teakiki

Riv. des Iroquois

R. Chianouché qui tombe dans la belle Riviere

75

60

Village de Poutouatamis

R. S. Joseph

Vill. de Poutoutamis Fort Pontchartrain Vill. de Hurons

R. S. Denis

R. aux Our

Natio

HUR

Natio

PA

L

The French advance into the interior of North America was led and directed by Samuel de Champlain. He reached the shores of Georgian Bay, the eastern arm of Lake Huron, in 1615, while others whom he sent out touched Michigan's shores by about 1620. No authentic portrait of Champlain exists, but there are several monuments, such as this one in Quebec, the city he founded in 1608, which honor Champlain as the "Father of New France." It was as a part of this colony that Michigan would first become acquainted with the white man and his ways.

In 1632 a map was published in Champlain's *Les Voyages de la Nouvelle France Occidentale* of which this is a section. Lake Huron (here called *Mer douce*) and Lake Superior (*Grand lac*) are shown, crudely to be sure, and they are connected by a series of rapids (*Sault*), to which the name Sault Ste. Marie would shortly be given.

Courtesy: William L. Clements Library

Courtesy: Public Archives of Canada

Courtesy: William L. Clements Library

During the course of his explorations, Champlain became involved in an Indian war, taking the side of Canadian tribesmen against the Iroquois Indians south of the St. Lawrence River in New York. With their guns, a weapon then unknown to the Iroquois, the few Frenchmen easily won the day for their allies, as shown in this contemporary sketch of the event. The skirmish had important consequences for Michigan, since it made the fierce Iroquois the implacable enemies of France. Rather than following the St. Lawrence-Great Lakes waterway system, which ran through Iroquois country, the French would move westward through central Ontario. Thus it was that northern Michigan, which lies directly west of the route through Ontario, became the first part of the state to be reached by the white man.

In 1641, two Jesuit missionaries, Father Isaac Jogues, shown here in a rare contemporary portrait, and Father Charles Raymbault, went from their Huron Indian mission at the head of Georgian Bay to the river that links Lakes Superior and Huron. Here, at the rapids which they named Sault de Sainte Marie, the Jesuit fathers met with the Indians of the area and conducted the first Christian services ever held on Michigan soil.

Courtesy: Collège Sainte-Marie, Quebec

27

Shortly after returning to their Huron mission, Father Jogues, Father Raymbault, and their colleagues and Indian converts were attacked by the Iroquois. In one of these attacks Father Jogues, who would be sainted by his church, was killed, an event depicted in a contemporary painting. It is appropriate that one of the Catholic churches in Sault Ste. Marie today honors with its name this Jesuit martyr.

The Huron Indians who survived the Iroquois onslaught fled westward to the distant shores of Lake Superior. An artist who illustrated Champlain's account of his explorations from 1615 through 1618 depicted members of this tribe in a rather romantic manner.

Eventually, when peace among the Iroquois and the French was temporarily restored, the Jesuits went west, seeking the remnants of the Christian Hurons. In the late 1600's, Father Jacques Marquette, shown here in a twentieth-century reconstruction of a faded painting on wood that is believed to be the only authentic surviving portrait of Marquette, served with these Indians near what is now Ashland, Wisconsin, as well as founding a mission at Sault Ste. Marie in 1668, which is the basis for the Soo's claim to being Michigan's oldest white settlement.

When the Huron Indians in the early 1670's again moved, this time east to the Straits of Mackinac, the Jesuits established a mission at this strategic point connecting Lakes Huron and Michigan. It was first located briefly on Mackinac Island in a bark chapel, similar to this one now seen on the island, a recent reconstruction based on seventeenth-century descriptions of such buildings.

Since the Indians helped the missionaries to build their missions, it was only natural that Indian building styles prevailed in these early mission structures. There are obvious similarities between the missionary's bark chapel and the bark- or skin-covered lodges of Michigan's Chippewa Indians, shown here in a sketch made in the nineteenth century by Lieutenant J. C. Tidball of the United States Army.

29

The first Jesuit known to have gone through the Straits of Mackinac to the west, however, was not Marquette but Father Claude Allouez who, for a quarter of a century before his death in 1689, carried on missionary work among the Indians throughout virtually the entire upper Great Lakes region. He lies buried at Niles, Michigan, where a Jesuit mission existed from the late 1680's to the 1760's. The traditional site of the grave of Allouez was marked by a wooden cross, as shown here in 1905. Later, in 1918, a local women's club erected a larger granite cross.

In 1671, Father Marquette established a permanent mission on the mainland of the Upper Peninsula opposite Mackinac Island. He named the mission after the founder of the Jesuit order, St. Ignatius of Loyola, and the modern city of St. Ignace, which grew up on this site, keeps this memory alive. Marquette Park, quiet and small, located just beyond the business section of St. Ignace, preserves what is thought to be the site of Marquette's mission. In the park, a few feet from the waters of the Straits of Mackinac, the avenue through which Marquette and his colleagues passed to seek out the lands and the Indians to the west, a modest monument, erected in 1882, marks the supposed spot where Marquette's bones were reburied in 1677, two years after he died somewhere along lower Michigan's western shore on his return from the Illinois country.

In addition to bringing the Christian religion to the Indians, the Jesuits in the course of their travels acquired a knowledge of the region which enabled them to make a major contribution to a better understanding of Michigan's geography. The best-known example is this Jesuit map of Lake Superior, published in 1672, which was the most accurate map of any of the Great Lakes until the nineteenth century.

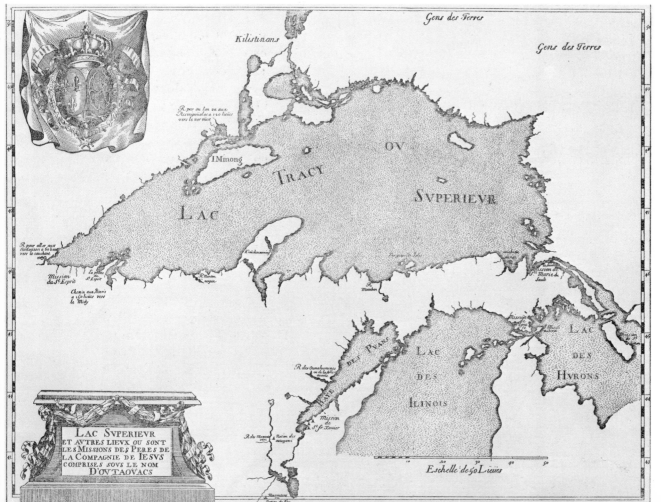

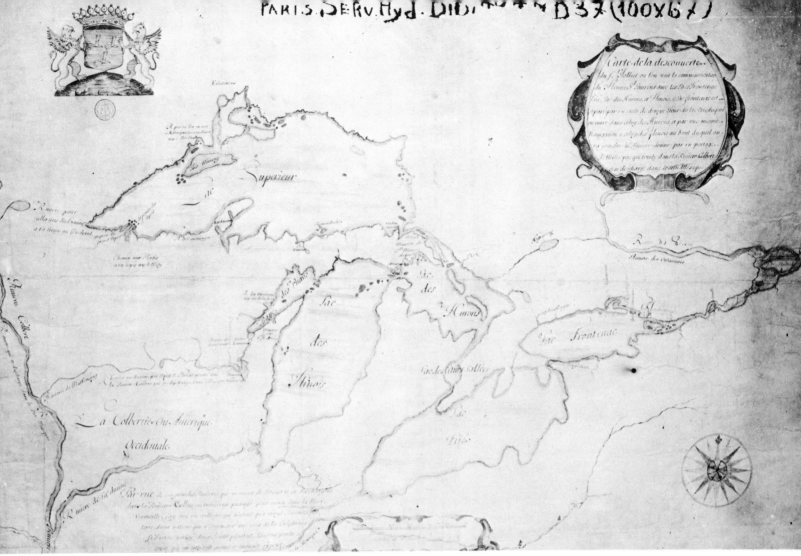

French exploration of Michigan and the Great Lakes was not confined to the Jesuits. Great names of lay explorers abound. Men like Louis Jolliet, who in 1673 went out from St. Ignace with Marquette on a journey of discovery to the Mississippi, and whose manuscript maps, such as this one, which Jolliet prepared upon his return, influenced European cartographers for many years.

A rival of Jolliet, and one of the most famous and controversial figures in the history of North American exploration, was René Robert Cavelier, the Sieur de la Salle. His exploits later would result in a statue of him ornamenting the exterior of the old Detroit City Hall for some ninety years. After the building was demolished in 1961, La Salle's statue (second from left), which was not an accurate representation since no authentic portrait of La Salle has been found, was stored away, along with statues of his fellow Frenchmen—Marquette, Father Gabriel Richard, and Cadillac— forgotten relics of an almost forgotten past.

31

As part of his grandiose plans to establish French outposts in the west, La Salle built the *Griffin,* the first sailing vessel on the upper Great Lakes, an event depicted by a contemporary European artist who illustrated the travel narrative of Father Louis Hennepin, who sailed westward with La Salle on the *Griffin* in 1679. The disappearance of the vessel in or near Michigan waters on its return voyage is one of the most intriguing mysteries in Great Lakes history.

Father Hennepin, shown here in a 1694 portrait, was a Recollect priest. The reliability of his narrative, particularly that dealing with what he claimed to have seen and done farther west, is debatable, but what he had to say about those parts of Michigan that he visited is both factual and interesting. Of the area that would become Detroit, he wrote: "Those who will one day have the happiness to possess this fertile and pleasant strait will be much obliged to those who have shown them the way."

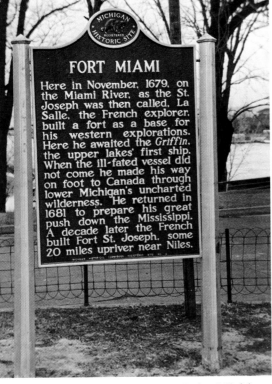

On a bluff overlooking Lake Michigan at the mouth of the river that later became known as the St. Joseph, where he had come after leaving the *Griffin* in Green Bay, La Salle erected a fort as a temporary base for his explorations to the west. It was the first French establishment of this type in lower Michigan. Like most other sites of French activity in Michigan, nothing remains today save a marker erected nearly three centuries later by the Michigan Historical Commission. Without it, the visitor to the old Whitcomb Hotel in St. Joseph, located across the street from the plaque, would scarcely guess that the land upon which the hotel stands was once occupied by a band of French adventurers.

The attraction for most Frenchmen who came to Michigan, however, was not adventure or geographical curiosity or missionary zeal. The prime magnet was a relatively small fur-bearing animal which, with a few other animals, was greatly valued in Europe for its pelt. The beaver, which is still found and hunted in Michigan today, thus became the first of Michigan's natural resources to be exploited by the white man.

A WOLVERINE.

The chaps from the Wolverine state, are the all-greediest, ugliest, an sourest characters on all Uncle Sam's twenty-six farms; they are, in thar natur, like their wolfish namesakes, always so etarnal hungry that they bite at the air, and hang their underlips, and show the harrow teeth of their mouths, as if they'd jump right into you, an swaller you hull, without salt. They are, in fact, half wolf, half man, and 'tother half saw mill. I met a wolverine one day in the forest, who had just swallowed a buck, an that war only enough to start his appetite, an make him al ravenous; he turned up his eyes at me, an opened his arth-quake jaws as if he war goin to chop off my head without axin. I chucked a lamb or two at him, but it war no more use than a hoss-fly to a buzzard. "Mr. Wolverine," says I, "you stare at me with a reg'lar cannibal grin, but darn me, if you mustn't fight before you can bite; my name's Crockett, an I'm an airthquake, and if the critter didn't draw up his under-lip, and fall to eaten off the bark of a tree, while his eyes watered along with his mouth, then take my whiskers for wolf skins.

A WOLVERINE.

Despite the dominant role of the beaver in Michigan's economy for some two centuries, it is one of history's ironies that Michigan has come to be associated not with that patient, hard-working animal, but with the wolverine, an ill-tempered beast whose habits have made his name synonymous with glutton, facts which help explain the fun which the *Davy Crockett Almanac* had with the subject in 1845. Actually, there is little evidence that wolverines have ever lived in Michigan, outside of zoos. Certainly, the value of wolverine pelts, wherever they came from, which were shipped from Michigan fur-trading posts was totally insignificant in the over-all picture.

33

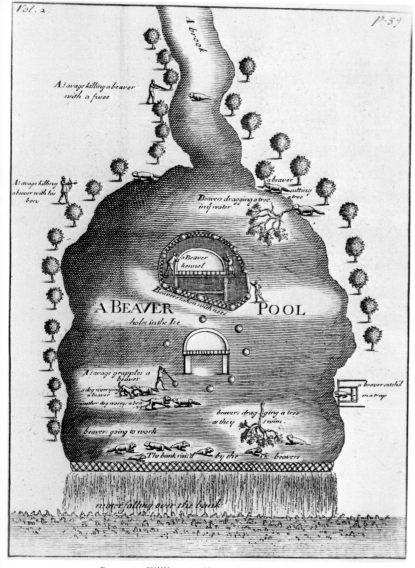

A savage killing a beaver with a snee

A savage killing a beaver with his bow

Beavers dragging a tree in the water

a beaver cutting a tree

a Beaver kennel

Beavers taken with nets

A BEAVER POOL

holes in the Ice

a beaver catch'd in a trap

A savage grapples a beaver

a dog worrying a beaver

another dog worrys a beaver

beavers going to work

beavers dragging a tree as they swim

The bank rais'd by the beavers

water falling over the bank

Courtesy: William L. Clements Library

An early eighteenth-century artist, illustrating the Baron de Lahontan's account of his travels in New France, including what is now Michigan, drew this rather fanciful picture of beavers industriously at work and Indians, on whose efforts the fur trader depended for his supply of furs, just as industriously killing and trapping the animals.

Lahontan, who was at the Straits of Mackinac in 1688, has left us a plan of this area, which was at that time the headquarters of the fur trade in the entire region of the upper Great Lakes. This copy of the plan, which appeared in the 1703 English edition of Lahontan's narrative, locates the mission at St. Ignace, the nearby settlement where the fur traders lived, and the villages of the Huron and Ottawa Indians. At the right-hand edge of the map is the tip of the lower peninsula, south of the straits connecting Lake Huron and what we now call Lake Michigan, but which was then commonly called the Lake of the Illinois. A few months after Lahontan left the straits, a fort was built at St. Ignace, although French soldiers had been sent there from time to time prior to the building of the post.

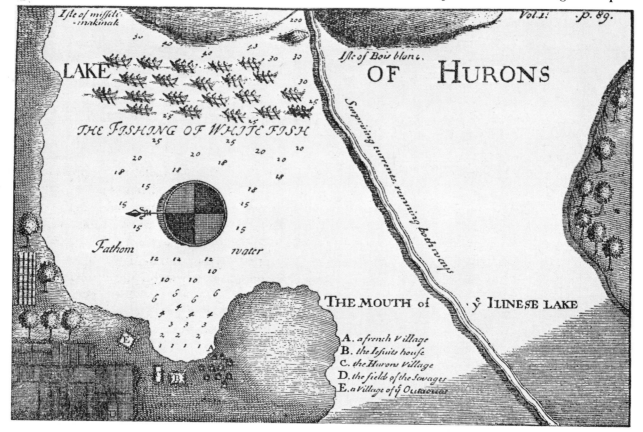

Isle of missilimakinak

LAKE

THE FISHING OF WHITE FISH

Fathom water

Isle of Bois blanc

OF HURONS

Surprising currents running both ways

THE MOUTH of ye ILINESE LAKE

A. a french village
B. the Jesuits house
C. the Hurons village
D. the field of the savages
E. a village of ye Outaouas

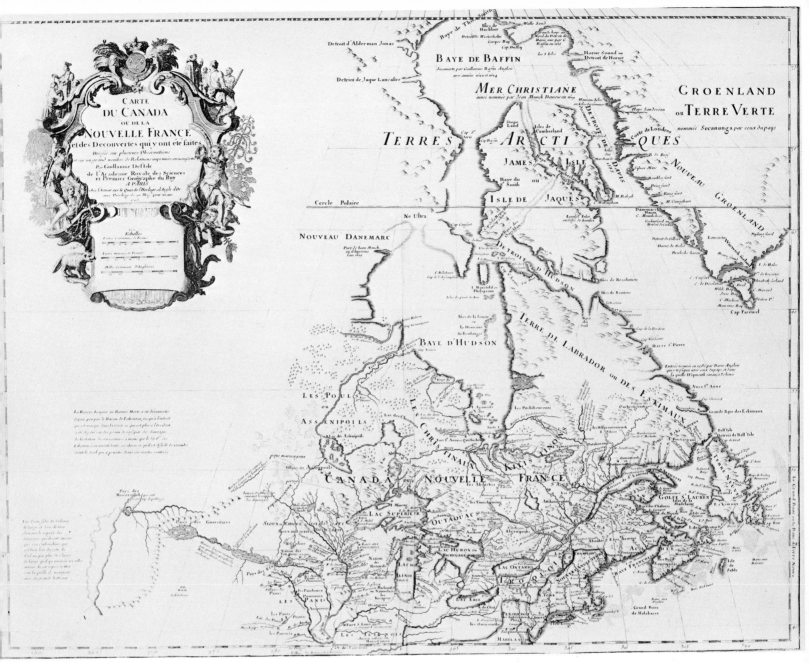

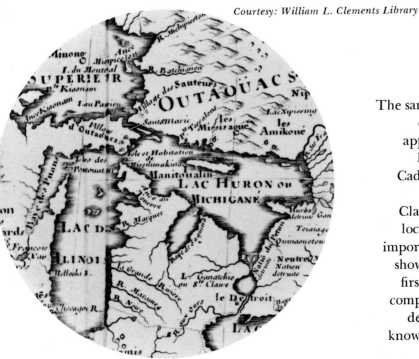

The same year, 1703, that Lahontan's map of the Straits of Mackinac appeared, a new name, Detroit, first appeared on a printed map. Michigan's largest city had its origin in 1701 when Antoine de la Mothe Cadillac established a settlement on the waterway or straits (*detroit*) linking Lake Erie with Lake St. Clair and ultimately with Lake Huron. Its strategic location made Detroit at once a post of pre-eminent importance in the fur trade. The map on which it was shown was the work of Guillaume Delisle, one of the first truly scientific cartographers, whose map, when compared with those of Champlain and Sanson, a few decades earlier, reveals the degree to which French knowledge of Michigan had been advanced by French exploration in the seventeenth century.

35

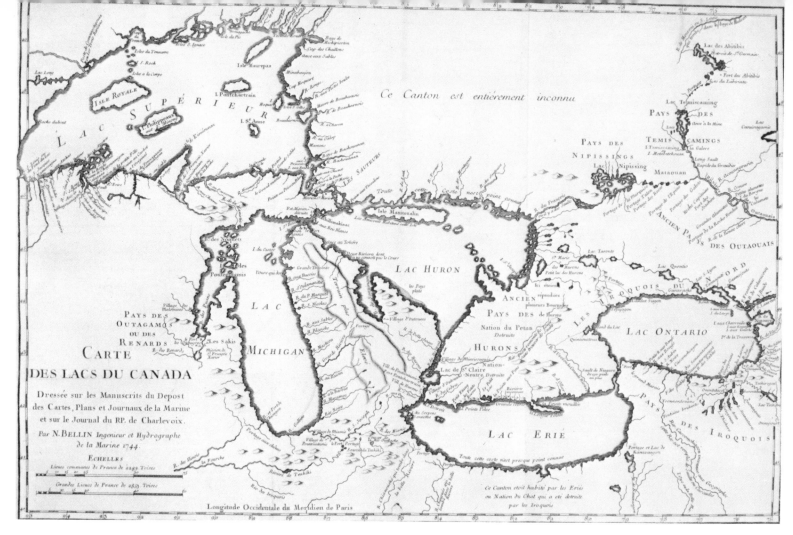

Strangely enough, an increased familiarity with the area did not guarantee increased accuracy in the maps of Michigan. Witness this well-known map of 1744, produced by a distinguished French geographer, Jacques Nicolas Bellin. It shows large islands in Lake Superior which no one before or since has ever seen, geographical errors which Bellin added to such other misconceptions of earlier eighteenth-century map makers as the fictitious ridge (*Terrain plus Elevé*) running up the center of the lower peninsula, and the southeasterly slant of Lake Michigan. All this despite the existence of the French missionary, military, and fur-trading posts which Bellin shows at the Sault, at Mackinac, on the St. Joseph River, and at Detroit (*Fort Pontchartrain*), some of whose inhabitants would certainly have spotted a few of Bellin's mistakes and distortions.

The French settlements shown on Bellin's map have long since vanished. What physical remains survive are, for the most part, buried beneath the modern cities of Detroit, St. Ignace, Sault Ste. Marie, and Niles. Fortunately, however, the site on the south side of the Straits of Mackinac to which the French in 1715 removed the fort which previously had been established at St. Ignace remained undisturbed and undeveloped for nearly two centuries after it was finally abandoned. Thus, in 1959 and in the years following, archaeologists from Michigan State University, the University of Michigan, and other institutions have been able to uncover the foundations and other traces of the fort's buildings and its stockade.

36

In 1963, the site of the Jesuit church, which, in the early 1700's, had also been transferred from St. Ignace across the straits to what is now Mackinaw City, was excavated. Each shovelful of sand and dirt was sifted through screen frames mounted on roller skates. Like gold miners examining the final contents of their pans for precious metals, the archaeologists search through the objects remaining behind on the screens, hoping to find items that to them are equally priceless, artifacts dropped or thrown away by their owners during the sixty-five years Fort Michilimackinac was occupied in the eighteenth century.

Among the items found within the fort were many that related to the religious activities that had been an important part of the life of the inhabitants during the French period. These included a crucifix, a Jesuit medal, and, very close to the church site, part of a bell, which could very well have been the bell that was rung to announce a church service.

In 1964, the Mackinac Island State Park Commission, the agency in charge of this state historic site, reconstructed the old Jesuit church on the original footings uncovered by the archaeologists, and in a style which was as faithful to that of the original as it was possible to make it from a study of the evidence found in the earth, in the few relevant historical documents, and the surviving architectural examples from the same period in French Canada.

Tens of thousands of artifacts have been uncovered in the excavation of Fort Michilimackinac. Much of it today appears to be junk or trash, which is precisely why it was tossed away two centuries ago. But a careful examination of these items reveals much about life in this frontier post, a life which, as the presence of such things as fine china indicates, was perhaps not as harsh as tradition tells us it was. (See also the two pictures at top of next page.)

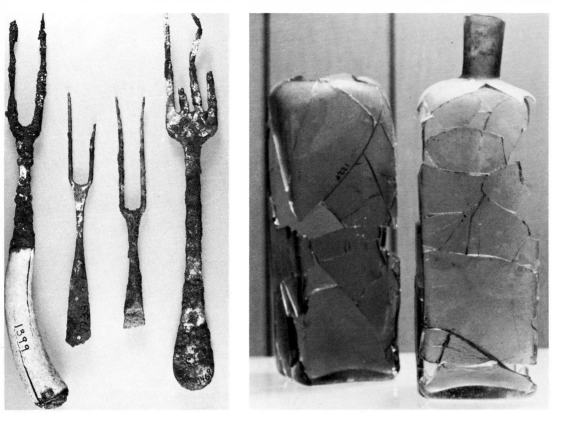

Gradually, Fort Michilimackinac is rising again from the sands along Lake Michigan, a lost page in the region's history that has been rediscovered.

Courtesy: Mackinac Island State Park Commission

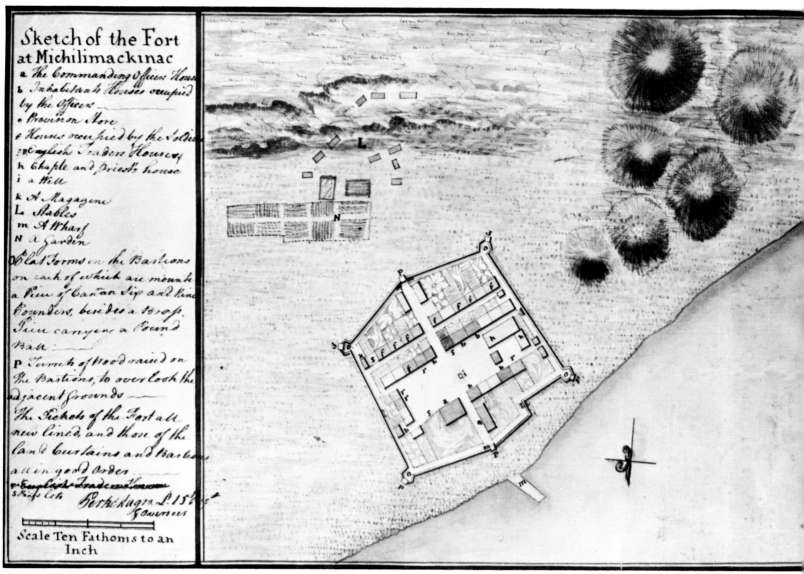

Courtesy: William L. Clements Library

Compare the outlines of the twentieth-century reconstruction with this plan of the fort, drawn in 1766. (The long narrow building which appears in the center of the fort in the aerial photograph is a reconstruction of the soldiers' barracks, which was not built until some years after the 1766 plan was prepared.)

40

The British Period

The plan of Fort Michilimackinac (p. 40) was drafted by Lieutenant Perkins Magra of the British army in 1766. A new era had begun five years before when members of Great Britain's 60th or Royal American Regiment had occupied Detroit, Michilimackinac, and the other posts in Michigan after the final surrender of the French holdings in Canada to the British. The change was dramatically documented when archaeologists at Fort Michilimackinac discovered these buttons from the uniforms of some of these soldiers.

No buttons were likely to be absent for long from the uniform of Major Henry Gladwin, who took over command of a garrison of Royal Americans at Detroit in 1762. Gladwin, whose portrait was painted later in life by the English artist John Hall, was an above-average example of the hardheaded, stolid, no-nonsense British officer, without whose devoted service the British Empire could never have been built or maintained.

Courtesy: Detroit Institute of Arts

Gladwin's assignment at Detroit was a difficult one. The stockaded fort where he and his men were stationed was built by Cadillac in 1701. It was actually a tiny walled city, with narrow streets, packed with buildings, as shown on this map which was published in 1764 but was based on surveys made between 1749 and 1755, when Detroit was still under French rule. The French soldiers had now departed, but the French farmers who resided up and down the river, outside the fort, still remained. They and the Ottawas, Hurons, and Potawatomies who lived in villages nearby looked upon the English as unwelcome intruders.

Courtesy: William L. Clements Library

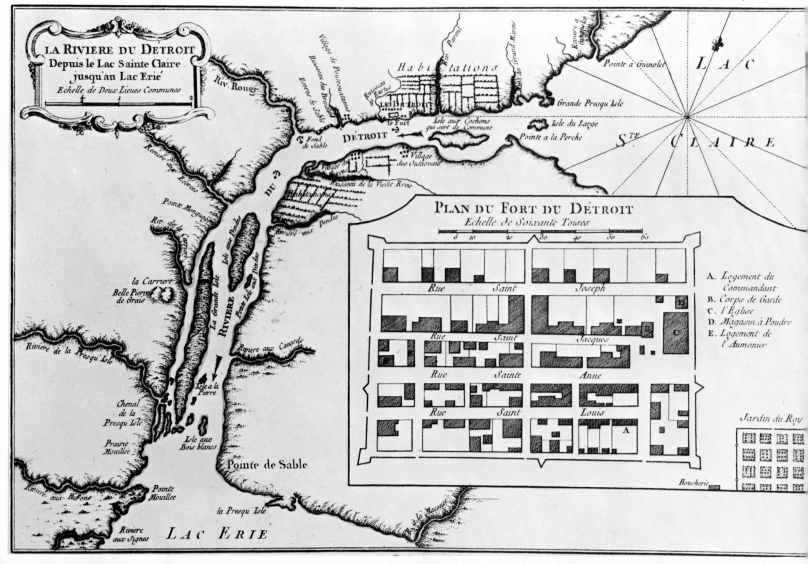

In 1763, the Indians in the Detroit area, led by a remarkable Ottawa chieftain, Pontiac, decided to capture the fort and expel the English. Today, in the sedate, sumptuously furnished William L. Clements Library at the University of Michigan, one can read Major Gladwin's report to his commander-in-chief, Sir Jeffery Amherst, in which he described how he foiled Pontiac's plot, forcing Pontiac to lay siege to the fort and thereby touching off the great Indian war that bears the Ottawa leader's name:

> On the first instant [May, 1763], Pontiac the Chief of the Ottawa nation, came here with about fifty of his men and told me that in a few days, when the rest of his nation came in, he intended to pay me a formal visit. The 7th he came but I was luc[k]ily informed the night before that he was coming with an intention to surprise us, upon which I took such precautions that when they entered the fort (tho they were by the best accounts about three hundred and armed with knives, tomhawks [sic], and a great many with guns cut short and hid under their blankets) they were so much surprised to see our disposition that they would scarcely sit down to council—however in about half an hour after they saw their designs were discover'd, they sat down and made several speeches, which I answered calmly without intimating my suspition [sic] of their intentions, and after receiving some trifling presents they went away to their camp—. This morning [May 7] a party sent by him [Pontiac] took Lieut. Robertson and Sir Robert Davers in a barge near

the entrance of Lake Huron, which Lieut. Robertson went to sound; they with the boat crew were all murdered. The 8th Pontiac came with a pipe of peace, in order to ask leave to come next day with his whole nation to renew his friendship. This I refused, but I told him he might come with the rest of his chiefs; however instead of coming the 9th in the afternoon he struck his camp and immediately commenced hostilities, by killing the Kings cattle and the people that took care of them, besides two poor english families that had settled in the country, he also cut off my communication with the inhabitants, and threatened them that the first that should bring me provisions or any thing else, he would put to death; they surrounded the fort and fired a vast number of shot at it and the vessels, which were anchored so as to flank the fort above and below. . . .

Gladwin goes on to relate the events of the following days, as Pontiac increased his pressure on the fort and Gladwin, in turn, refused the Indians' demand that he surrender. He concluded his report to Amherst by declaring, in the best traditions of the British army:

We are in high spirits and have provisions and ammunition enough to serve us till a relief arrives. I believe the enemy may amount to six or seven hundred. I have the honor to be Sir your most humble servant Henry Gladwin.

44

Courtesy: Ferris Lewis

On July 31, a sortie against the Indians, led by Captain James Dalyell, ended in disaster for the English soldiers. In what is now Detroit's Elmwood Cemetery, along a stream which ever since has been called Bloody Run, Pontiac and his warriors ambushed Dalyell's men, killing Dalyell and many more of the soldiers, wounding and capturing still others, and forcing the survivors to fight their way back to the safety of the fort.

Despite Pontiac's victory at Bloody Run, he was unable to maintain an effective siege of Fort Detroit since he could not prevent supplies and reinforcements from being brought in to Gladwin from the river. Finally, at the end of October, with winter approaching and his Indians anxious to return home, and with the receipt of news that all hope of French military aid must be abandoned, Pontiac, who could not write, dictated this note to Gladwin, whom he addressed as "My Brother":

> The word which my father [the French authorities] has sent me to make peace I have accepted. All my young men have buried their hatchets. I think you will forget the bad things which have taken place for some time past. Likewise I shall forget what you have done to me, in order to think nothing but good. . . .

Pontiac's siege of Detroit, the longest Indian military operation of this character in American history, had come to an end.

Courtesy: William L. Clements Library

45

Courtesy: Mackinac Island State Park Commission

Pontiac's attack upon Detroit was followed in a few days by attacks by Indians elsewhere on every English outpost in the West. On June 2, 1763, outside the stockade at Fort Michilimackinac, a seemingly innocent game between the Chippewa and Sac Indians suddenly turned into a murderous assault on the unsuspecting English garrison, resulting in the capture of the fort by the Indians and in every Englishman at Michilimackinac either being killed or taken prisoner. Today, when the gate beneath this gun platform is opened, tourists, not hostile Indians, pour in, walking over the very ground on which took place what has gone down in history as the "Massacre of Fort Michilimackinac." White men wrote this history. To the Indians, it was a great victory that they had won at Fort Michilimackinac.

Courtesy: William L. Clements Library

Among the Englishmen at Michilimackinac who were captured was the fur trader Alexander Henry, shown here in his prosperous later years in Montreal. The intervention of a friend whom Henry had made among the Chippewas saved him from death at the hands of the enraged savages. It was this ability of the English fur trader to establish amicable relationships with the Indians plus the need of the Indian for the trader and his trade goods that helped put an end to the Indian war of 1763.

46

CAPTAIN GRANT,

Informs the Traders at Michilimakinack, Detroit, *and* Niagara.

THAT he will tranfport their Merchandize in the Veffels on the Lake, at the following Rates:

New-York Currency.

From Ontario to Niagara, a three handed Boat, or 12 Barrels; the Diftance about 170 Miles, £ 6 - 0 - 0

From Fort William Auguftus, per Barrel, to Niagara; the Diftance about 300 Miles, 7 - 0 - 0

From Niagara to Detroit, a three handed Battoe Load, or 12 Barrels, exclufive of the Carrying-Place; the Diftance about 300 Miles, 12 - 0 - 0

From Detroit to Michilimakinack, a three handed Battoe, or 12 Barrels; the Diftance about 400 Miles, 12 - 0 - 0

All other Things will be tranfported in Proportion to the above, and nothing charged for any fmall Articles in a Battoe, over the 12 Barrels.

FREIGHT OF PACKS, &c.

From Michilimakinack to Detroit, per Pack, — — — — — £ 0 - 4 - 0

From Detroit to Niagara, exclufive of the Carrying-Place, — — 0 - 4 - 0

From Niagara to Ontario, each Pack, — — — — — 0 - 2 - 0

From Niagara to Fort William Auguftus, per Pack, — — — — 0 - 4 - 0

The veffels (wind and weather permitting) will fail from Ontario the 10th of May, and 1ft of September, and from Fort Erie, the 20th of May and 20th of September; as alfo at any other times when there is fufficient freight; and from Detroit to Michilimakinack, when moft convenient for thofe who may have effects to fend there. The veffels arriving from Ontario, will difcharge at the Lower Landing, and at Little Niagara boats and men will be found to tranfport the goods and packs, to, and from, Fort Erie, gratis. The utmoft care will be taken of every thing fent, and proper ftores provided at Fort Erie. The mafters of veffels will fign bills of lading for any merchandize that are fhipped on the above conditions. As no charge will be taken at the Carrying-Place, at Niagara, every owner of goods, muft provide a careful perfon to take charge of their effects at that place. By adopting this manner of conveyance to the feveral pofts, the property of an Indian trader, and his credit (of courfe) with his merchant, will become infinitely lefs liable to hazard than in that of proceeding fingle and defencelefs in fmall open boats, which fubjects them to be feized by the Savages, who thereby become poffeffed of ammunition and cloathing, that may enable them to carry on a long feries of hoftilities againft our pofts and fettlements; an event of the moft mifchievous tendency to the Britifh government, deftructive of human life, and which would produce a train of calamities horrible to be reflected on, yet ever to be apprehended from the uncertain duration of peace with our troublefome neighbours.

The English developed the fur trade in Michigan considerably beyond the level to which the French had brought it. For the first time since the ill-fated voyage of the *Griffin,* sailing vessels appeared on the upper Great Lakes, making it possible to bring trade goods to Detroit and Michilimackinac more efficiently, economically, and safely than by canoe or *batteau.* These advantages were pointed out in this advertisement in the Quebec *Gazette* for March 22, 1770, one of the earliest examples of the advertising man's art applied to Michigan.

Courtesy: Quebec Provincial Archives

Courtesy: Minnesota Historical Society

Despite the use of sailing vessels, the heavy work of the fur trade under the English continued to be handled by the French *voyageur.* It was these men, one of whom was portrayed by Mrs. Samuel B. Abbe in the mid-nineteenth century, whose arms and backs provided the muscle needed to propel the fur traders' *batteaux* over the hundreds of miles of lakes and rivers that had to be traveled to obtain the furs from the Indians. The *voyageur* also provided the brute strength required to portage boat and cargo around the numerous rapids and overland to the next waterway.

But the men who enjoyed the enormous profits of the fur trade were not the *voyageurs* or the Indians, or, for the most part, the traders who went out and obtained the pelts. It was the men at Michilimackinac and Detroit who hired the traders and *voyageurs*, and especially the men back in Montreal who provided the capital that profited from the trade. Such a man was James McGill, one of the Montreal entrepreneurs who was closely connected with the Michigan fur trade in the last four decades of the eighteenth century and whose name today is perpetuated in McGill University, Montreal, endowed with the fortune he made in the business.

During these years of British rule, the land which would become Michigan continued to be governed by military men. As a group, these officers were less colorful than Cadillac, La Salle, and some of the others from the earlier French period. One redcoat who, although he may have lacked judgment, certainly did not lack color, was Major Robert Rogers, founder of Rogers' Rangers and the central figure in Kenneth Roberts' great novel, *Northwest Passage*. It was Rogers who had established British authority at Detroit in 1760 and had fought at Bloody Run during Pontiac's siege before he was named to head the garrison at Michilimackinac in 1766. Two years later he left the post under arrest, charged with "Designs of a Traiterous and Dangerous nature" against his king and his country. Although he was acquitted of the charge, Rogers' career was effectively ruined. This portrait, although published in 1776 during Rogers' lifetime, has been labeled fictitious, an attempt by the artist, Thomas Hunt, to cash in on the desire of the British public to secure copies of a likeness of the notorious officer.

A few years after the ignominious departure of Rogers from his Michilimackinac command, an officer of a very different, but likewise unusual, character took over at that post. Arent Schuyler de Peyster was a member of a distinguished New York colonial family, who, in later years, would retire to Scotland where he became a friend of the poet Robert Burns. This was a natural development, since De Peyster can be termed Michigan's first literary figure. He spent the long, boring hours at the Straits of Mackinac in composing poems. In 1779, about a year before this portrait was made, he was transferred to Detroit. He rose to the occasion with this lyric:

> *Now to Mitchilimackinack*
> *We soldiers bid adieu,*
> *And leave each squa a child on back,*
> *Nay some are left with two.*
> *When you return, my lads, take care*
> *Their boys don't take you by the hair,*
> *With a war-whoop that shall rend the air,*
> *And use their scalping knives.*

Courtesy: Burton Historical Collection

As Major de Peyster and his men were en route to Detroit in 1779, other British soldiers were locked in combat with the American colonists along the Atlantic seaboard. There was scant sympathy for the revolutionists among the English and French residents of Michigan, and yet, among the items uncovered in the archaeological excavation of Fort Michilimackinac is this political button honoring the English liberal and friend of the colonists, John Wilkes. Was its owner simply a collector of such trivia, or was he an admirer, if not an adherent, of the American cause, proclaiming his sentiments in a bastion of British military might?

Courtesy: Mackinac Island State Park Commission

Courtesy: Burton Historical Collection

Although far removed from the battlefields, Detroit and Michilimackinac played an important role in the war in the West, for it was at these posts that parties of Indians were organized to raid the American frontier. Henry Hamilton, who, in 1775, was named commander at Detroit and the first lieutenant-governor of the Detroit District in the enlarged province of Quebec, directed these campaigns. He was labeled "Hair Buyer" by the Americans for his action in paying the Indians for scalps. Historians have since proved that the Americans were being unjust to Hamilton, but whether deserved or not, Hamilton's nickname has been responsible for keeping his name alive in Michigan history when officers of equal or greater rank have long since been forgotten.

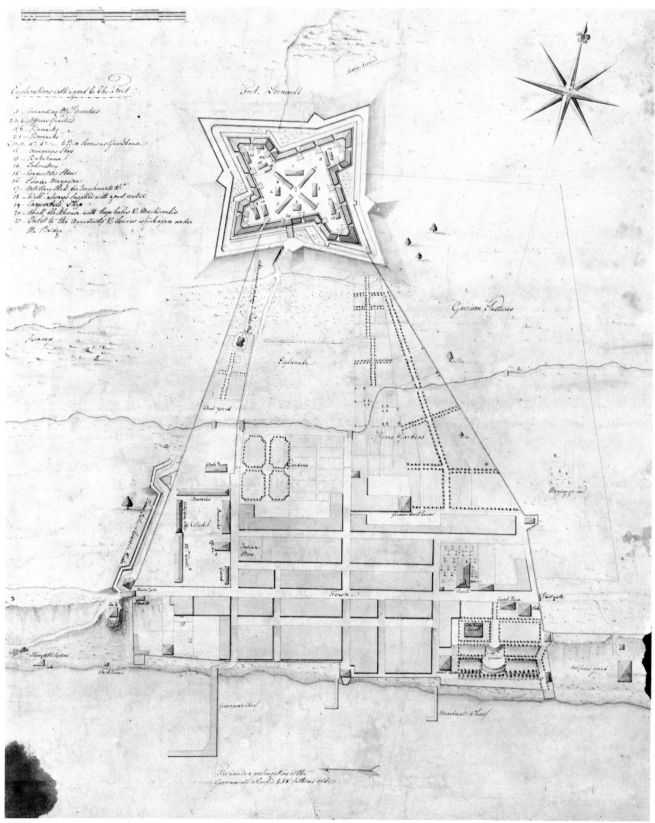

During the Revolution, the British, fearing American attacks in reprisal for the raids launched from Michigan, moved to strengthen their military positions. At Detroit, a new fort, named Fort Lernoult, was built in 1778-79, some distance inland from the old French fort site on the banks of the Detroit River. This map, drawn in 1799 by John J. Rivardi, shows how the new fort was connected with the town of Detroit to the south.

Detroit's central business district has been built on the ruins of eighteenth-century Detroit — a fact dramatically demonstrated in 1962 during the construction of a skyscraper addition to the Detroit Bank and Trust building at Fort and Shelby. The contractors suddenly struck something that was subsequently determined to be the remains of Fort Lernoult's southwest bastion. Work was halted on the twentieth-century building while archaeologists from Wayne State University, headed by Dr. Arnold Pilling, carefully uncovered the timbers of a structure that had stood on the same site two centuries earlier. A treasury of artifacts was rescued for later study after the construction crews had resumed their work on top of Fort Lernoult's reburied ruins.

51

Meanwhile, back in 1779, De Peyster had been replaced at Michilimackinac by Captain Patrick Sinclair, shown here in a silhouette made in his later years of retirement in his Scottish homeland. Sinclair, who in 1764 had brought the first sailing vessel up Lake Huron to Mackinac since the voyage of the *Griffin* eighty-five years earlier, had been named lieutenant-governor of the Michilimackinac District in 1775 but the war had delayed his arrival in northern Michigan until 1779.

Courtesy: Burton Historical Collection

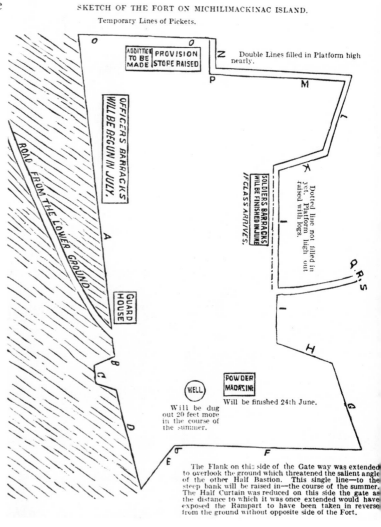

SKETCH OF THE FORT ON MICHILIMACKINAC ISLAND.
Temporary Lines of Pickets.

Double Lines filled in Platform high nearly.

ADDITION TO BE MADE
PROVISION STORE RAISED

OFFICERS BARRACKS WILL BE BEGUN IN JULY.

SOLDIERS BARRACKS WILL BE FINISHED IN JUNE IF CLASS ARRIVES.

Dotted line not filled in yet. Platform high raised with logs. out

ROAD FROM THE LOWER GROUND

GUARD HOUSE

WELL
Will be dug out 20 feet more in the course of the summer.

POWDER MAGASINE
Will be finished 24th June.

The Flank on this side of the Gate way was extended to overlook the ground which threatened the salient angle of the other Half Bastion. This single line—to the steep bank will be raised in—the course of the summer. The Half Curtain was reduced on this side the gate as the distance to which it was once extended would have exposed the Rampart to have been taken in reverse from the ground without opposite side of the Fort.

Deciding that the post on the northern tip of the lower peninsula was too vulnerable to an attack by Americans or Indians, Sinclair, in the fall of 1779, laid out the plans for a new fort across the straits on Michilimackinac Island (as Mackinac Island was called until well into the nineteenth century). This is a late nineteenth-century reproduction of a sketch of the work on the new fort from British records. The reproduction was made before the modern era of photo-duplication techniques which have enabled an exact copy of manuscript drawings and plans to be made.

Unlike Fort Lernoult, which was built at the same time but was later demolished in the 1820's, Sinclair's Fort Mackinac, as it would be called, survives today. In the Fort Mackinac which one now sees, however, as in this aerial photograph in which the fort appears in the left center as a pie-shaped cluster of buildings, scarcely any of the structures date from Sinclair's day.

Courtesy: Mackinac Island State Park Commission

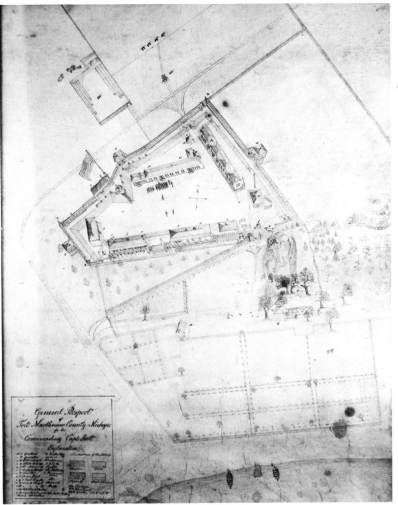

Courtesy: William L. Clements Library

Not even this bird's-eye view, prepared by an American soldier in the early 1840's, contains much that the builders of the original fort would have recognized.

The impressive limestone escarpment, pierced by the South Sally Port, facing out over the harbor of Mackinac Island, probably dates from the early 1780's, although it has had to be repaired many times in the succeeding years.

Inside the fort, only the architecturally acclaimed Officers' Stone Quarters dates from Fort Mackinac's days as a British post, but even it was not completed by Sinclair or his successors. It remained for the Americans in the late 1790's to add the roof.

Courtesy: Historic American Buildings Survey

Courtesy: Historic American Buildings Survey

Likewise, the fort's famed blockhouses, probably the most photographed man-made structures in Michigan, were apparently built by the Americans in the late 1790's and, despite what the guidebooks have been saying all these years, do not date from 1780.

With the transfer of British troops to Fort Mackinac, the old fort on the mainland to the south was abandoned. Gradually this historic post disappeared before the ravages of time and shifting sands. By 1842, when this sketch was made, passengers on ships passing through the Straits of Mackinac could see no sign that the site had been inhabited only sixty years earlier.

Courtesy: Michigan Tourist Council

Courtesy: Chamber of Commerce of Greater Niles

Neither Fort Mackinac nor Fort Lernoult was attacked during the American Revolution, but in Niles a huge boulder and a historical marker locate the site of Fort St. Joseph which, on February 12, 1781, was briefly occupied by forces of Spain, which then controlled the area west of the Mississippi River and had entered the war as an ally of the Americans. It was an easy triumph for the Spaniards because the fort had not had a British garrison in eighteen years.

Today the Four Flags Motor Inn (formerly the Four Flags Hotel) in Niles helps to keep alive an aspect of that city's history in which it takes great pride—it is the only Michigan community over which the flags of four nations, France, Great Britain, Spain, and the United States, have flown.

Courtesy: William L. Clements Library

In 1783 the Treaty of Paris ended the American Revolution. Great Britain recognized the independence of its rebellious colonies along the Atlantic and agreed upon the boundaries of the new United States of America. This map, published by John Wallis of London on April 3, 1783, less than three months after the treaty went into effect, was one of the first maps of the new country to be rushed into print. Although Wallis obviously was not well informed as to the location of the northwestern boundary, to the residents of Michigan the map made one thing clear: Michigan had become American.

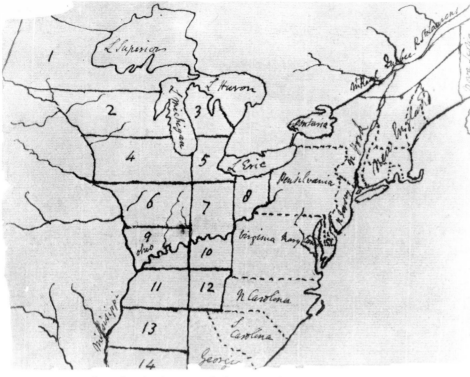

The United States government lost no time planning for the development of its western lands. In 1784, Congress passed an ordinance, prepared by Thomas Jefferson, in which the great Virginian proposed the creation of ten states in what is now the Middle West. Jefferson, with customary imagination, even named the states, and on this manuscript map showed their approximate boundaries. Most of what is now Michigan would have been included in Jefferson's states of Cherronesus (3) and Sylvania (1). Jefferson named one of his states Michigania, number 2 on his map, but it would have been confined primarily to the present state of Wisconsin. Jefferson's ordinance was never put into effect, but he had, nonetheless, set in motion a chain of events that eventually would result in the establishment, twenty years later, of a political division to which the name Michigan would be applied.

The Ordinance of 1784 was replaced in 1787 by what many historians regard as the most important act ever passed by any Congress, the Northwest Ordinance, establishing the Northwest Territory. This territory, which was delineated by Joseph Scott of Philadelphia in his *United States Gazetteer* of 1795, included the future states of Ohio, Indiana, Illinois, Wisconsin, a portion of Minnesota—and all of what would become the state of Michigan.

56

Getting title to Michigan's lands and waters was one thing, but getting actual possession was something else. The Americans had to deal with the British, who refused to leave until the Americans fulfilled certain conditions of the treaty of 1783. The Americans also had to deal with the Indians of the Great Lakes region, who did not recognize the right of any white man to give or take lands which the Indians regarded as their own. Only in 1795, after several years of difficult, costly fighting, did the United States Army get some of

Courtesy: Chicago Historical Society

these Indians to agree to relinquish their claims to most of Ohio and to narrow strips of land at Detroit and the Straits of Mackinac. An American soldier who was present at this historic event in Greenville, Ohio, is believed to be the artist who portrayed officers and chieftains negotiating the treaty.

Courtesy: Burton Historical Collection

General Anthony Wayne, the stern, tall officer in the painting, was the officer who organized and directed the defeat of the Indians, and who dispatched the American troops that finally occupied Michigan in 1796, the year in which this portrait was painted and the year in which he met his untimely death.

Anthony Wayne himself visited Detroit in the fall of 1796 to help set up American civil authority—and appropriately enough, the first county established was named in his honor. This is how Wayne would have seen Detroit as he looked up the Detroit River at the old fort on the river bank, standing about where Cobo Hall now stands. An unknown artist made this wash drawing in 1794, when the British flag still flew over the stockaded post and the royal naval vessels anchored in the river.

Courtesy: Burton Historical Collection

In 1804, a British army doctor, Edward Walsh, stood on the Canadian side of the Detroit River, in what is now Windsor, Ontario, and made this sketch of Detroit, over which the United States flag now waved.

Later in 1804, Walsh added a painting of the fur-trading posts at the rapids of the St. Mary's River, what is now Sault Ste. Marie, Michigan, and its sister community across the international boundary, Sault Ste. Marie, Ontario.

On the American side at Sault Ste. Marie, a Scotsman, John Johnston, maintained a trading post. He and his Chippewa wife, Susan or Ozha-Gus coday, had a remarkable progeny whose descendants today are found scattered through Michigan and elsewhere in the country and have included in their numbers some prominent individuals. Johnston, however, although he was now technically an American, remained loyal to the British, as did a great many more of the residents of Michigan who stayed on in the area after 1796. This would prove to be a serious problem for the American authorities, which was not resolved for many years.

South of Sault Ste. Marie, on St. Joseph Island at the head of Lake Huron, Dr. Walsh visited the fort and trading establishment which the British had built in 1796 when they finally had to evacuate the fort on Mackinac Island, some forty-five miles to the west.

Mackinac Island, shown here in an engraving published in 1813, continued under American control as an important fur-trading center. A small settlement hugged the shoreline of the harbor, while on the high ground overlooking the waterfront a small force of soldiers represented American authority in this most remote northern United States military outpost.

The year 1805 is one of the most important in Michigan's history, for it was at that time that Congress established a new territory in the northwest and called it Michigan. Now for the first time it was possible to refer to a political unit and a land area that bore this name. As is shown by Amos Bradley, Jr., of Philadelphia, in this map that is dated 1804 but apparently was actually printed in 1805 or later, the boundaries of Michigan Territory in 1805 were not the same as those of the present state. Only the eastern tip of the Upper Peninsula was part of the new territory.

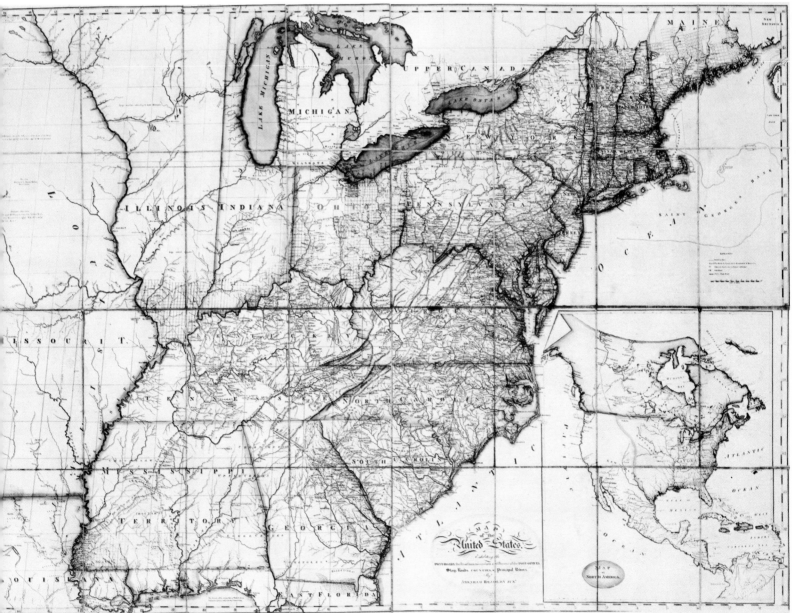

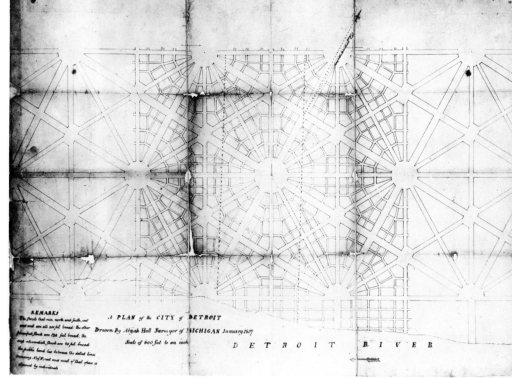

REMARKS

A PLAN of the CITY of DETROIT

Drawn By Abijah Hull Surveyor of MICHIGAN January 1807

Scale of 600 feet to an inch

D E T R O I T   R I V E R

Left: William Hull, a 52-year-old New Englander and veteran of the Revolution, was selected by President Thomas Jefferson to be Michigan's first governor. This portrait was painted by Gilbert Stuart, probably in 1824, a short time before Hull's death. In the 1960's it was owned by Hull's great-great-granddaughter, Mrs. James E. R. Jones of Lakeville, Connecticut.

Right: When Governor Hull arrived in Michigan in the summer of 1805, he found that most of Detroit, the territorial capital, had been destroyed by a great fire on June 11. In the most forward-looking action of Hull's administration, a plan for rebuilding Detroit, drawn up by Judge Augustus B. Woodward, was adopted by the territorial government.

Below: Woodward's plan, an adaptation of the one prepared for Washington, D. C., by Major Pierre L'Enfant, was later abandoned by citizens who could see no need for two-hundred-foot wide avenues and numerous circular parks. Twentieth-century Detroit, however, as this 1930 aerial photograph reveals, still retained a few traces that Judge Woodward would have recognized. Had his plan been adhered to, Detroit might have been spared some of its monstrous traffic headaches of the past few decades.

Hull and Woodward represented the American wave of the future, but for some years the majority of the territory's white population would continue to be, as it had been since Champlain's day, French-speaking. Representing this element was a remarkable priest from France, Father Gabriel Richard, who came to Michigan in 1798, and although based at Detroit, was responsible for the Catholics throughout the entire upper Great Lakes region. He served the area in a variety of capacities until his death in 1832 from cholera, which he contracted while helping others during an epidemic that swept southeastern Michigan. This portrait was painted shortly after Richard's death by the artist James O. Lewis, and was based upon his examination of the dead man. Lewis was paid twelve dollars for what would become one of the most widely reproduced portraits ever made of a Michigan resident.

Courtesy: Burton Historical Collection

Father Richard was more than just another priest, faithfully serving the needs of his French Catholic parishioners. He was interested in many things that looked to the cultural and political development of Michigan. He imported a printing press, one of the first in Michigan, on which were produced some of the rarest, most sought-after Michigan imprints, including Michigan's first newspaper, the *Michigan Essay*. Michigan apparently was not ready for a newspaper, however, because there is no evidence that any other issues followed this initial issue of August 31, 1809. The Burton Historical Collection of the Detroit Public Library has one of the few known copies of this issue.

Governor Hull, although not an outstanding chief executive, did make at least one major contribution to the territory's subsequent development when in 1807 he negotiated a treaty with the Indians for the cession of their lands in southeastern Michigan. The northern boundary of the area ceded began near the town of Harbor Beach at a famous landmark in Lake Huron known then—and now—as White Rock.

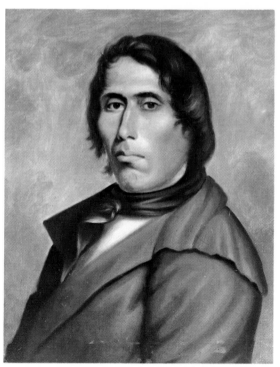

Opposition to the advance of American settlers into the West led some Indians to plan a united resistance to this movement. Some authorities believe that this portrait, whose origin is uncertain, is one of the leader of these Indians, Tecumseh, a Shawnee who lived in Indiana but whose influence with many Michigan Indians at this time was great. Ironically, a Michigan town in Lenawee County would be named in his honor by admiring white men of a later generation, the very people whose further intrusion into Indian country Tecumseh had fought against. Similarly, descendants of Pontiac's enemies would name a town, a lake, and an automobile after that earlier foe of the English-speaking white man.

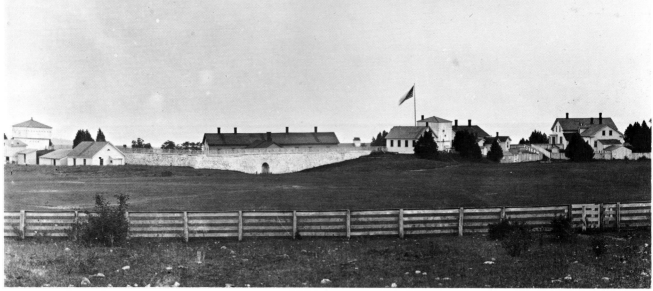

Courtesy: Al Barnes

The feeling of the Western frontiersman that the British in Canada were inciting Tecumseh in his anti-American activities and that they were behind other Indian problems in the West was a primary cause of the War of 1812—a war which broke over Michigan in all its fury in the summer of 1812. On the night of July 16-17, a British force from St. Joseph Island quietly landed on the north end of Mackinac Island and by morning had occupied the high ground to the rear of Fort Mackinac, shown here in a late nineteenth-century photograph.

Courtesy: Mackinac Island State Park Commission

Courtesy: Hiram Walker Museum

The American garrison of some sixty men had not yet learned that war had been declared. Faced by an overwhelmingly superior force, including hundreds of Indians who might massacre civilians on the island if a fight were made, the commander of the fort surrendered without a struggle and marched his men out of the fort through this North Sally Port.

Meanwhile, at Detroit, Governor William Hull had been given command of the American army in the northwest, with orders to invade Canada. He crossed the Detroit River and took up quarters in this brick house, then owned by François Baby, now a museum in Windsor maintained by the Hiram Walker Company.

By WILLIAM HULL, *Brigadier General· and Commander of the North Western Army of the United States.*

A PROCLAMATION.

INHABITANTS of CANADA! After thirty years of Peace & profperity, the United States have been driven to Arms. The injuries & aggreffions, the infults & indignities of Great Britain have *once more* left them no alternative but manly refiftance, or unconditional fubmiffion. The Army under my command, has invaded your country, & the Standard of the Union now waves over the Territory of Canada. To the peaceable unoffending inhabitant, it brings neither danger nor difficulty. I come to *find* enemies, not to *make* them. I come to *protect*, not to *injure* you.

Separated by an immenfe Ocean, & an extenfive Wildernefs from Great Britain, you have no participation in her Counfels, no intereft in her conduct. You have felt her Tyrany, you have feen her injuftice, but I do not afk *you* to avenge the one or to redrefs the other. The United States are fufficiently powerful to afford you every fecurity, confiftent with their rights, & your expectations. I tender you the invaluable bleffings of Civil Political & Religious Liberty, & their neceffary refult individual and general profperity; That Liberty which gave decifion to our counfels and energy to our conduct, in our ftruggle for Independence, and which conducted us fafely and triumphantly, thro' the ftormy period of the Revolution. That Liberty which has raifed us to an elevated rank among the Nations of the world, and which has afforded us a greater meafure of Peace and Security, of wealth and improvement, than ever fell to the lot of any people.

In the name of my *Country* and by the authority of my *Government*, I promife you protection to your *perfons, property* and *rights*. Remain at your homes. Purfue your peaceful and cuftomary avocations. Raife not your hands againft your brethren. Many of your fathers fought for the freedom & Independence we now enjoy, Being children therefore of the fame family with us, and heirs to the fame heritage, the arrival of an Army of friends, muft be hailed by you with a cordial welcome. You will be emancipated from Tyrany and oppreffion, and reftored to the dignified ftation of freemen. Had I any doubt of eventual fuccefs, I might afk your affiftance, but I do not. I come prepared for every contingency. I have a force which will look down all oppofition, & that force is but the vanguard of a much greater. If contrary to your own intereft, and the juft expectation of my Country, you fhould take part in the approaching conteft, you will be confidered & treated as enemies, & the horrors & calamities of war will ftalk before you.

If the barbarous & favage policy of Great Britain be purfued, and the favages are let loofe to murder our Citizens, & butcher our women and children, this war, will be a war of extermination.

The firft ftroke of the Tomahawk, the firft attempt with the fcalping knife, will be the fignal for one indifcriminate fcene of defolation. *No white man found fighting by the fide of an Indian, will be taken prifoner.* Inftant deftruction will be his lot. If the dictates of reafon, duty, juftice and humanity cannot prevent the employment of a force which refpects no rights, & knows no wrong, it will be prevented by a fevere and relentlefs fyftem of retaliation.

I doubt not your courage and firmnefs : I will not doubt your attachment to Liberty. If you tender your fervices voluntarily, they will be accepted readily.

The United States offer you Peace, Liberty and Security. Your choice lies between thefe & War, flavery, and deftruction. Choofe then, but choofe wifely ; and may he who knows the juftice of our caufe, and who holds in his hand the fate of Nations, guide you to a refult the moft compatible with your rights and intereft, your Peace and profperity.

BY THE GENERAL

Capt: 13th. U. S. Regt: of Infantry and Aid de camp.

Hull issued a proclamation to the Canadian people, printing it on the press Father Richard had brought to Detroit. The bombastic tone of the message was in striking contrast to Hull's naturally cautious personality. Actually, he was fully aware of the weaknesses in his position which limited his ability to carry out his threats.

Downriver from Detroit, on the Canadian side, the British had military and naval forces at Fort Malden, which they had built in 1796 after they were forced to evacuate Detroit. The town of Amherstburg, the fort, and the navy yard are shown on the right and Bois Blanc Island (today's popular Bob-Lo summer amusement center) on the left in this painting made in 1813 by Catherine Reynolds, sister of the fort's commissary. One of the Indians in the lower right-hand corner is supposed to be Tecumseh, who was now openly supporting the British.

In August, Sir Isaac Brock, military commander of Upper Canada (present-day Ontario), arrived at Fort Malden with reinforcements. A career military man, General Brock not only had the edge on his opponent, Hull, in the matter of experience but also in the ability to make and to execute command decisions.

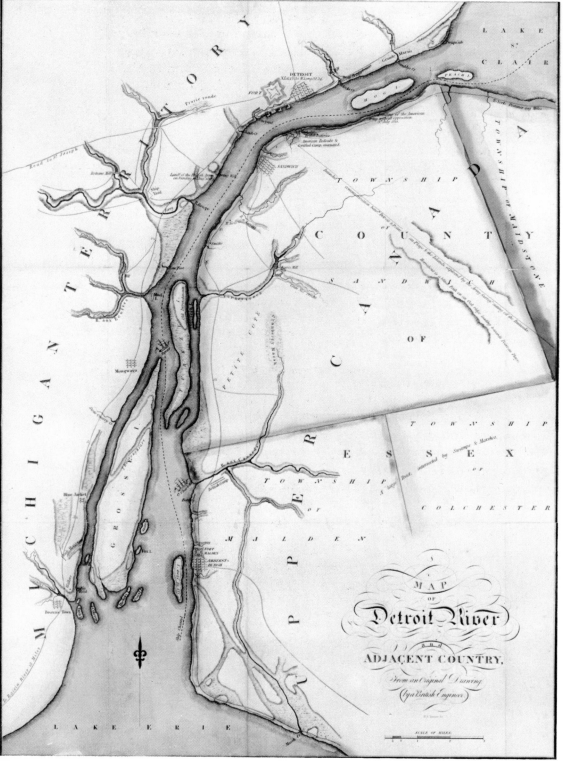

What happened on the Detroit River in July and August, 1812, is clearly shown on this map, published the following year and based on a drawing by a British engineer. From his positions on the Canadian side of the river, opposite Hog Island (today's Belle Isle), Hull had sent scouts probing as far south as the Canard River. But efforts to bring supplies overland up the American side of the river from the River Raisin were frustrated in battles between American troops and Indians led by Tecumseh and his British allies at Browns Town (in the modern community of Gibraltar) and in the area of the Indian village of Mongwaga (now the city of Trenton). This inability to bring supplies, plus British naval control of the Detroit River, and finally news of the fall of Mackinac Island and Brock's imminent arrival, caused Hull to abandon invasion plans and to pull back to the defenses of Detroit. The British and American artillery batteries on the opposite shores of the river engaged in a spirited duel on August 15. The following morning, Brock and his men crossed the river below Detroit, quickly advanced up the river road, and, at noon, Hull, fearful of what Britain's Indian partisans might do to the civilians living around Detroit, accepted Brock's demand that he surrender. Hull's career in Michigan thus came to an inglorious end. He departed as a prisoner of the British and he would later be made a scapegoat by the American government for the disasters it suffered early in the war.

PROCLAMATION.

By ISAAC BROCK *Efquire, Major General, Commanding his* MAJESTY'S *forces in the Province of* UPPER CANADA. *&c. &c. &c.*

WHEREAS, the Territory of MICHIGAN was this day, by *Capitulation*, ceded to the arms of His BRITANNICK MAJESTY, without any other condition than the *Protection* of private property. And wishing to give an early proof of the moderation & Juftice of the Government, I do hereby announce to all the INHABITANTS of the faid Territory that the laws heretofore in exiftence fhall continue in force until His MAJESTY'S pleafure be known, or fo long as the peace & fafety of the faid Territory will admit thereof. And I do hereby alfo declare & make known to the faid INHABITANTS that they fhall be protected in the full exercife & enjoyment of their RELIGION, of which all perfons both civil & military will take notice & govern themfelves accordingly.

All perfons having in their poffeffion or having any knowledge of any Public property, fhall forthwith deliver up the fame or give notice thereof to the Officer Commanding or Lt. Col. Nichol who are hereby duly authorized to receive & give proper receipts for the fame.

Officers of Militia will be held refponfible that all arms in poffeffion of Militia men be immediately delivered up : And all individuals whatever who have in their poffeffion arms of any kind will deliver them up without delay.

GIVEN under my hand at Detroit the fixteenth day of Auguft 1812, & in the fifty fecond year of His MAJESTY'S reign.

ISAAC BROKE,

MAJOR GENERAL,

Detroit—and Michigan—was again under British control, as this proclamation by Isaac Brock, coming from the same press that but a month before had printed Hull's proclamation to the Canadians, made perfectly clear.

More disasters lay ahead for the Americans. At the little settlement of Frenchtown, as Monroe was then called, near the mouth of the River Raisin, an American expedition which had come up from Ohio to protect the settlers was itself surprised and overwhelmed on January 22, 1813. The British marched their captives back to Fort Malden, but left behind a number of wounded Americans. Many of the latter were killed on January 23 by Indians who were enraged at the losses they had suffered in the fighting on the previous day. This graphic wartime print helped to make the cry, "Remember the River Raisin," an effective means of rallying Westerners throughout the remainder of the war.

In the summer of 1813, the tide of the war turned in the Americans' favor. At Put-in-Bay, a few miles east of Michigan in Lake Erie, Captain Oliver Hazard Perry led a new American navy to victory over the British fleet in the decisive battle of the war and one of the most important in American history.

Perry sent this terse report of his victory to the American authorities. The phrase "We have met the enemy and they are ours" was enough to make the young New Englander one of the most frequently quoted American heroes.

The American victory on Lake Erie forced the British to abandon Detroit. American forces, commanded by General Duncan McArthur of Ohio, who had commanded a regiment that served with Hull in 1812, reoccupied Michigan's principal city on September 29, 1813. The authority of the American government had been restored, this time permanently, to southeastern Michigan.

The war in Michigan did not end with the reoccupation of Detroit, however. In the summer of 1814, troops commanded by young Lieutenant-Colonel George Croghan were sent north up Lake Huron to recapture Fort Mackinac.

Before attacking Mackinac Island, the Americans had several secondary objectives, including John Johnston's fur-trading post at Sault Ste. Marie, which was partially burned in retaliation for aid which Johnston had given the British. Johnston's home, which he built probably a year or so later, is preserved as a historic house museum in the Soo. Some of the construction details, such as the hand-cut laths, are exposed to view in the interior.

When the expedition reached Mackinac Island, the Americans found that it would be impossible to launch a frontal assault on Fort Mackinac. When Croghan sought to accomplish his goal by landing on the north side of the island, away from the fortifications on the south side, he ran into an ambush on Michael Dousman's farm where a strong British and Indian force drove the Americans back with considerable losses. Mackinac Island and all of northern Michigan only returned to American hands in 1815, after the treaty ending the war.

In the summer of 1815, the British garrison at Fort Mackinac packed its bags and moved to a new fort built a few miles to the northeast on Drummond Island, which the British believed to lie on the Canadian side of the international boundary. Here they could continue to exercise an influence over the Great Lakes Indians, some of whom are shown in the early 1820's rendezvousing on Drummond Island to receive gifts from the British. The buildings of the British fort are in the distance, behind the Indian encampment along the shore.

But in 1822, a British-American commission surveyed the international boundary through the lakes and decided that Drummond Island should be placed in American territory. Not until 1828, however, did the British finally leave the island. Today, stone chimneys are about all that survive of Fort Colyer, the last British-held military post on Michigan soil.

The Passing of the Old Michigan

In the fall of 1813, a young, vigorous Yankee arrived in Michigan to be the new governor of the territory. Lewis Cass, shown here in a rare youthful portrait of undetermined date by Abraham G. Tuthill, would be the dominant political force in Michigan for the next half-century. A New Hampshire native who had begun his political career in Ohio as a Jeffersonian Democrat, Cass had come to Detroit in 1812 as commander of one of Hull's regiments. His impatience with Hull's cautious conduct of the war had reached the point of outright mutiny. Now during the eighteen years that Cass would be governor of Michigan, this same quality would help him to become an energetic administrator who, more than anyone else, would be responsible for changing Michigan from a remote wilderness possession inhabited by a few Indians, fur traders, and government employees, to a booming area swarming with people who were hurrying to take up the rich lands in the southern part of the territory.

During the early part of this period, Governor Cass resided in this house. It reportedly dated from the early 1700's, having survived the fire of 1805. Scars of bullets which had struck the building during Pontiac's siege were still visible when Cass moved in. The house was torn down in 1882; thereby one of the last remaining ties was removed which linked Detroit, rapidly advancing into the modern world, with its historic French past.

This house, which Cass built in 1840, some years after he sold his first Detroit home, was a good example both of Cass's prosperity and of the progress Michigan had made since 1813. The house, which was located at Cass and Fort Streets in Detroit, was removed in 1876—a quick casualty of Detroit's accelerating growing pains.

At the same time that the new Michigan of the farmer and tradesman was emerging under the aegis of Governor Cass, the old Michigan of the fur trader, the Indian, and the soldier enjoyed one final fling. In the decade or so after the War of 1812, the American Fur Company, organized from New York by the German immigrant John Jacob Astor, enjoyed a complete monopoly of the fur trade in the United States.

Under Astor's American company, as earlier under the British and French trading companies, the backbone of the business was supplied by the French-Canadian *voyageurs* who formed the crews of canoes which took the trader and his goods to the distant Indian villages. This painting, *circa* 1870, was the work of Mrs. Frances Anne Hopkins, who depicted three traders' boats moving through a Lake Superior fog. Mrs. Hopkins knew her subject, since she had frequently accompanied her husband on trips that he had made as an agent for the Hudson's Bay Company.

Mackinac Island in these years was the hub of the fur trade for the Great Lakes and regions to the west. This painting by an unknown primitive artist of the period conveys some of the excitement that characterized life on Mackinac in the heyday of the fur trade.

Astor's trusted aide on Mackinac Island was Ramsay Crooks, who used up-to-date techniques to bring greater efficiency than ever before to the centuries-old fur-trading business, and rooted out competitors with a ruthlessness that any business tycoon of the late nineteenth century would have viewed with admiration.

During a few weeks each summer, hundreds of clerks labored in the buildings of the American Fur Company on Mackinac, keeping a record of millions of dollars' worth of furs which the traders had brought in. Two of these buildings have survived over the years. In the late nineteenth century they were joined together and put to a different use, as a popular resort hotel, the John Jacob Astor House. In the present century the buildings were restored to their original condition, with one of them, named the Stuart House, after Ramsay Crooks' long-time associate at Mackinac, Robert Stuart, being operated as a historic house museum. The buildings, probably the oldest surviving commercial structures in Michigan, are good examples of the classical style of architecture which was the fashion in the East in the early nineteenth century and which Americans brought with them when they emigrated to Michigan.

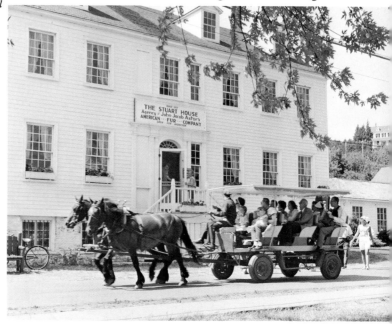

Courtesy: Historic American Buildings Survey

Courtesy: Michigan Tourist Council

Down the street from the American Fur Company buildings was, and is, a modest house which is believed to be the oldest private residence on Mackinac Island, if not in Michigan. Its architectural style and mode of construction hark back to those that were popular in Michigan's pre-American period. Houses similar to it are still found in rural Quebec Province. The house was purchased in the 1820's by Edward Biddle, who was involved in the fur trade and in other island business and political activities for many years. The Biddle House ceased to be occupied in the 1930's, was boarded up, and its fate hung in the balance until it was restored in the late 1950's by interested architectural and construction groups.

In the 1820's and 1830's there were scattered through Michigan numerous trading posts that were subsidiaries of the operations at Mackinac. In the Grand River valley, Astor's agent during these years was Rix Robinson, a native of Massachusetts, who exemplified the high caliber of many of Astor's men. An educated man of great ability, Robinson was married twice, each time to an Indian woman, a fact which contributed to the great influence he had over the Indians around what is now Grand Rapids. Later in life, when he posed for this photograph, he became a potent political figure in western Michigan.

Courtesy: Jack T. Crosby, Jr.

On Grand Island, just off the
Upper Peninsula in Lake Superior,
these cabins stood until the
1960's, relics of a small trading
post built on the island in the
early nineteenth century. The
buildings were later converted to
use as summer cottages. Finally,
when this latter use had been
abandoned, some of the historic
cabins, with their squared-log
walls and stone fireplaces, were
removed to other locations off
the island or were threatened with
final destruction.

Abraham W. Williams, a native of Burlington County, Vermont, operated the Grand Island post for many years. He lies buried on the island in an unkempt little graveyard, tucked away in a wilderness setting. This is appropriate, since he made his living from pelts of forest creatures. When he died, the forests remained, but the great fur trade had long since moved far to the west, ahead of the wave of settlers who swept into Michigan, disrupting the old patterns upon which the fur trade had been built.

Symbolic of the change that took place in Michigan in the 1820's and 1830's is the historic Mission Church on Mackinac Island, shown here in a photograph taken in the early twentieth century. Built in 1829-30, it was part of a Protestant Indian mission which also provided services for the increasingly large non-Catholic white population on the island. It is the oldest surviving church building in Michigan. As its Federal-style architecture and its austere interior suggest, its builders were Yankees from New England and New York. These were men who, like their Puritan forefathers, might be interested temporarily in trading and working with the Indians, but who ultimately looked to acquiring the land for themselves and to developing farms and settlements and all the other features of the culture and civilization in which they had been raised.

By 1842, the Indians of Michigan, through a series of treaties with the United States government, had ceded away their claims to all their lands with the exception of a few small areas reserved for their use. For a few years after signing these treaties, the Indians received annual payments from the government agents. A British visitor, Colonel Henry Ainslie, made this fine sketch of Mackinac Island, showing the Chippewa encampment at the time of the annual payment of 1842.

The government agents, of whom Henry Rowe Schoolcraft is Michigan's best known, worked with the dispossessed Indians and were charged with the supposedly desirable objective of aiding these native Americans in adapting to the ways of the white man.

Schoolcraft in the 1820's worked at Sault Ste. Marie, where the Indian Agency House, which dates from that decade, is still preserved.

At Mackinac, where Schoolcraft moved in the 1830's, a dormitory was built to provide a place where Indians having business on the island might stay, protected by the agent from the traders in the village, some of whom used liquor to take unfair advantage of the Indians. Few of the Chippewas and Ottawas who came to the island used the dormitory, and eventually it was used as a schoolhouse for ten times the length of time it was used as an Indian dormitory.

78

The full nature of the tragedy that had befallen the Indian now became increasingly clear. The independent native of the prehistoric era, living or dying by his own wits, the Indian of the fur-trading era, who, although he was more and more dependent on the white man, retained some measure of pride by the fact that he was the principal source of supply for an item highly valued by the white man—these were no more. In their place now were pitiful figures such as Chief Okemos, reputedly a leading aide of Tecumseh during the War of 1812, who in his last years in the 1850's was a familiar character in Lansing, where he and his tribesmen were reduced to cadging drinks from the white man.

Courtesy: Hartford Public Library

The policy of the federal government in the 1830's was to remove the Indians east of the Mississippi to new lands in the West, away from the flood of settlement that was sweeping over the regions of the Middle West and the Deep South. Some Potawatomi Indians in southwestern Michigan were removed to what later became Kansas, but Michigan's Indians as a whole escaped this fate and were allowed to remain in the state. They survived as best they could under difficult circumstances. Some achieved a certain kind of fame. Leopold Pokagon, whose portrait, painted in 1838, is owned by the Northern Indiana Historical Society, was the leader of a group of Catholic Potawatomi Indians living in Cass and Berrien Counties, who were exempted from the removal policy. Leopold's children, particularly Simon, added more luster to what was probably Michigan's best-known Indian family. . . .

Courtesy: Ray Brotherton

. . . Chief Shoppenagon, shown posing with his wife and young daughter, was well known for many years to visitors in the Grayling area where he served in various capacities, and many a hunter and salesman has stayed in the hotel in Grayling that bears his name. . . .

. . . Indian dress continued to be worn by some Indians, such as the sad-eyed young girl, Full Moon, but many did so now because it was what the tourist and the photographer expected of them . . .

. . . More and more Indians adopted the white man's dress and ways, with more or less success as, for example, those in the Charlevoix area who, in the mid-nineteenth century, built a little log Methodist church at Greensky Hill, where they and their descendants have worshipped ever since. . . .

. . . But for many others, the problems of adjustment, compounded by the white man's neglect and prejudice, led only to the poverty which was the lot of the Indian family standing outside its cloth-covered dwelling on the shores of Lake Superior, opposite Grand Island, in 1870, . . .

Courtesy: Marquette County Historical Society

... or the Indian fish dressers standing outside their log hut at Whitefish Point, late in the century.

Until the end of the nineteenth century, vestiges of the frontier military fort continued to be found in Michigan, as they had since the 1600's. General Hugh Brady, who built a fort at Sault Ste. Marie that bore his name, and who served in Michigan well into his seventies, was in the tradition of Cadillac and Gladwin—guarding the frontier from the Indian.

As late as the 1840's, a traditional stockaded wooden fort was built at the tip of the Keweenaw Peninsula. A sketch of the fort, called Fort Wilkins, appeared in 1846 in a unique handwritten camp journal, *The Agate. . . .*

Courtesy: Michigan Tourist Council

. . . Supposedly the fort was built to protect the copper miners who were swarming into the area from the Indians, but many have speculated that the garrison actually was intended to protect the Copper Country's hapless natives from the miners. At any event, the need for troops to be stationed at the fort, which is now a state park, was short-lived.

In the late nineteenth century, soldiers continued to drill, . . .

Courtesy: Mackinac Island State Park Commission

. . . perform guard duty, and go through the rest of the military routine at Fort Mackinac, but with the passing of the fur trade and the Indian danger the post had long since become an anachronism. The last garrison was evacuated in 1895, and the fort was turned over to Michigan as part of the first state park.

Courtesy: Mackinac Island State Park Commission

In the 1830's the Detroit Arsenal was built, oddly enough, not in Detroit, but ten miles to the west in what is now Dearborn. It was an arms depot designed to supply the military posts throughout the Old Northwest. With the passing of the frontier and the closing down of many of these posts, the need for the arsenal decreased, until finally it was abandoned in 1877. Today, the one-time headquarters of the arsenal's commandant serves as the headquarters of the Dearborn Historical Museum. *Courtesy: Dearborn Historical Commission*

Courtesy: Historic American Buildings Survey

In the late 1840's, Fort Wayne was built at Detroit. Some of its buildings, such as the massive barracks, contrasted sharply with the smaller and simpler structures of Michigan's earlier forts. The reason is easily determined. Fort Wayne was not intended to be a frontier post but a military base in the settled part of the country, where the troops were trained in peacetime and in times of war were assembled and transported to the areas of military action.

The Coming of the Pioneers

Late in 1836, tragedy struck the family of J. and A. Darling, who lived in western Wayne County. Louesa, a daughter not yet two years old, died on December 1. Six and a half years later, Louesa's brother Charles, aged seven years and six months, also died. None of the Darling family became famous. Rather, history files the family away, along with tens of thousands of others, under the heading "Pioneers." Louesa and Charles Darling are buried in a tiny, rural cemetery on a bank overlooking US-12, which in pioneer days was the Chicago Road, one of the main routes west out of Detroit. A stone, now much weathered, gives probably as much information about these children as we will ever have. Similar graveyards, often neglected and overgrown, are scattered by the hundreds throughout Michigan, with grave markers whose inscriptions may now be illegible, if the markers themselves are not broken or fallen over. But the real monuments to the Darlings and their fellow pioneers are the farmlands which they cleared and the villages and towns and cities they founded.

In the late 1800's, some pioneers set down their reminiscences as they looked back over their lives and recognized how they and their contemporaries had, in a few years, altered the entire appearance of southern Michigan. Among the best-known memoirs are those of William Nowlin, which he recorded in *The Bark Covered House,* published, as were so many of these historical works, in the year of the nation's centennial, 1876. Illustrations, drawn, presumably, under the watchful eye of the author, depict the stormy passage of the Nowlin family in 1834 from New York in the steamboat *Michigan;* . . .

. . . the tavern whose proprietor was hired by the Nowlins to move them from Detroit over the Chicago Road to the land John Nowlin had purchased in Dearborn; . . .

. . . the bark-covered log cabin which was the Nowlin's first home; . . .

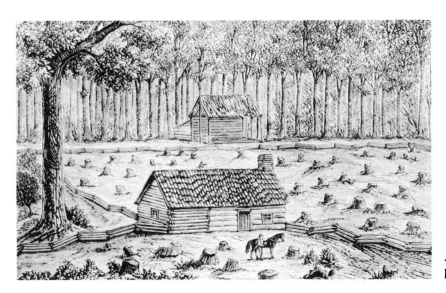

. . . the larger house which they built in 1836; . . .

... the rapid development of the area, symbolized by the coming of the railroad to Dearborn in 1837; ...

... and finally the well-cleared, fenced acres of the Nowlin farm, with its barns and its three-story brick house, built in 1854, "not as palatial as some might admire, but a good substantial house." The series of illustrations effectively summarize the problems and triumphs of the successful pioneers of the middle decades of nineteenth-century Michigan.

Before the Nowlins or anyone else could legally settle in Michigan, the land, after it had been relinquished by the Indians, had to be surveyed by federal surveyors. This tremendous task of literally walking over the entire surface of Michigan and marking township and section corners at half-mile intervals began in earnest in 1815 and was substantially completed by 1850. Lucius Lyon, one of the most prominent of those who carried out this project, started as a young surveyor in Michigan in the 1820's, gaining a knowledge which he used to good advantage subsequently in a variety of real estate promotions, including the town of Lyons and a large section of what would become Grand Rapids. Lyon also served as one of Michigan's first two United States senators before returning to his earlier profession as surveyor general for Ohio, Indiana, and Michigan.

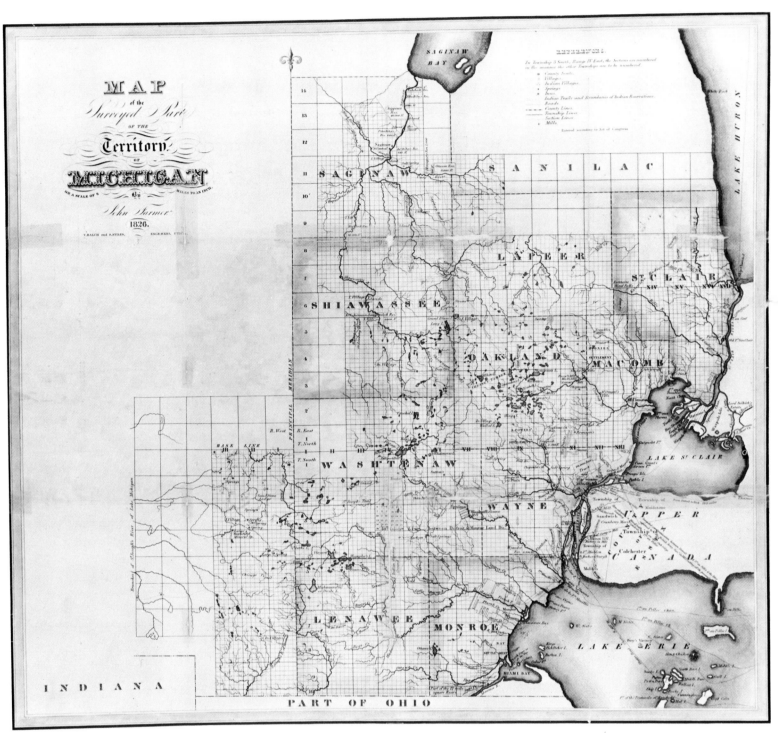

By the mid-1820's, the surveyors had carried out their task across the southeastern part of the lower peninsula, as shown on this 1826 map, which was one of the first maps produced by John Farmer, the founder of Michigan's most famous map-making firm which continued in business into the twentieth century. The difference between the American system of surveying the land into neat square sections measured off from the Principal Meridian running north and south, and the east-west Base Line (the origin of today's Meridian Road in Ingham County and Base Line Road along the Wayne County-Oakland County boundary), and the earlier French system, under which lots were laid out at ninety-degree angles to the rivers, is graphically illustrated by examining the pattern along the Detroit River and the River Raisin which had been settled in the eighteenth century.

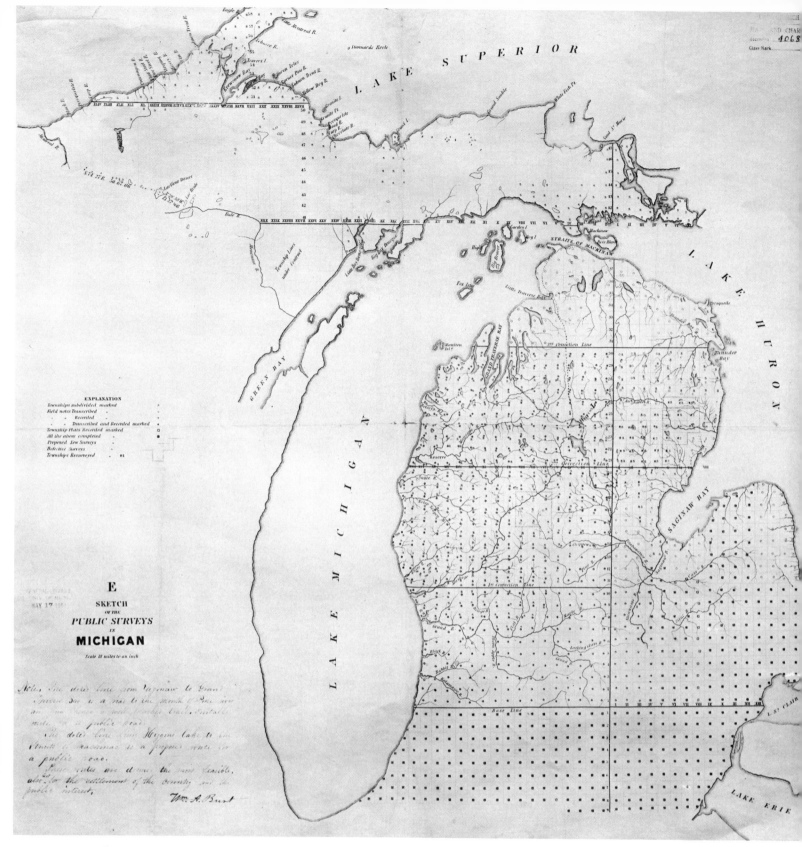

By about 1847, the federal survey of Michigan was well on its way to completion, as indicated on this map, which shows that by this time the job was completed in southern Michigan, the field work was virtually completed in the rest of the lower peninsula, while in the Upper Peninsula a good start had been made on laying out the townships. William A. Burt, who probably did more of the land survey than any other single individual, includes a note on this map that the dotted lines running from the Saginaw valley up to Grand Traverse Bay and the Straits of Mackinac indicated the best routes for roads into these areas which were still almost totally unsettled.

90

Surveyed land could be purchased from United States land offices, the first of which was opened in Detroit in 1818, a second a few years later in Monroe, and a third in 1831, at White Pigeon, the first land office in western Michigan. This office was moved to Kalamazoo in 1834, but the building in which it was housed while in White Pigeon is believed to be a dilapidated structure now occupied by a restaurant. The land office buildings at Detroit and Monroe are not known to have survived.

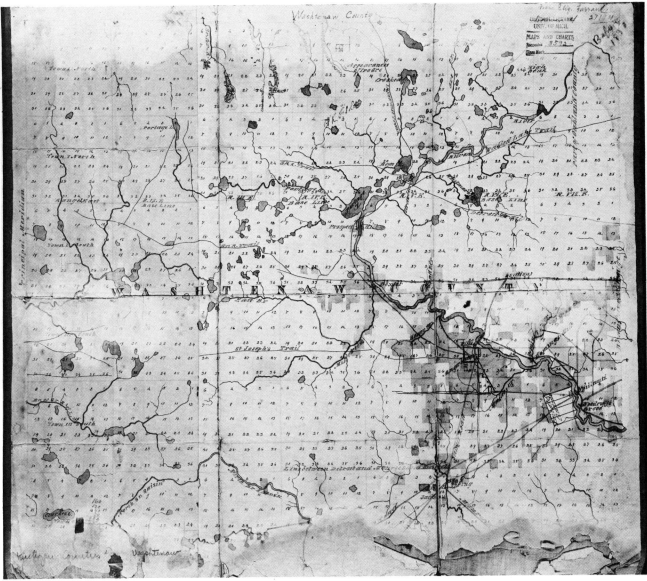

Courtesy: University of Michigan General Library

At the land office, the seeker after public land, whether a prospective settler or a speculator, could quickly learn if the section he was interested in was still available. On this Washtenaw County map from the late 1820's, those lands around Ypsilanti and "Anarbour" which had been taken up were shaded in a solid color by a land office employee. The non-shaded areas were still for sale at the low, low price of $1.25 an acre. Later, after the passage of the Homestead Act in 1862, over three million acres of land were obtained in Michigan by homesteaders who paid nothing except a small registration fee, if they had resided on the land for five years.

called *Lac des Illinois*; is fifteen miles long, of an oval figure, and subject to a flux and reflux.

SURFACE, SOIL, TIMBER.

There are no mountains in this territory; the interior is table land, having a western and northern inclination, interspersed with small lakes and marshes, from which issue the head branches of the rivers. Prairies exist, from the banks of the St. Josephs to lake St. Clair; some are of an excellent soil; others, sandy, wet and sterile. There are, nevertheless, extensive forests, of lofty timber, consisting of oak, sugar maple, beach, ash, poplar, white and yellow pine, cucumber, buckeye, basswood, hickory, cedar, plum, crab apple, cherry, black and honey locust. The last flourishes as far north as the margin of lake Huron—yet east of the Allegany mountains, it is never found north of the Delaware. The bottoms, and high prairies are equal to those of Indiana. A considerable part of the coast of lake Michigan consists of a range of sand-hills, thrown up by the surf and "eddying winds." The timbered uplands are well adapted to the production of most kinds of grain; and appear to bear a long series of crops, as is the case with the ridge in the rear of Detroit.

EXTENT OF CEDED LANDS.

At a treaty held at Detroit in November, 1807, between Gen. Hull and the chiefs of the Pottawattamie, Ottawa, Wyandot, and Chippawa tribes, all the lands within the following limits, except the reservations hereafter described, were ceded to the United States, viz: "Beginning at the mouth of the Miami river of the lakes, and running thence up the middle thereof, to the mouth of the great Au Glaize river; thence running due north until it intersects a parallel of latitude, to be drawn from the outlet of lake Huron, which forms the

Courtesy: Michigan Historical Collections

Land sales in Michigan proceeded at a very slow pace for a number of years. The great Michigan land boom, one of the most spectacular in American history, did not come until the mid-1830's, nearly two decades after land in Michigan first went on the market. Despite a legend that has persisted for many years, this delay was not the result of unfavorable publicity. Actually, reports of Michigan soil were overwhelmingly favorable, as, for example, these comments from Samuel R. Brown's *The Western Gazetteer; or Emigrant's Directory*, published at Auburn, New York, in 1817.

On August 27, 1818, the *Walk-in-the-Water* completed its first trip from Buffalo to Detroit. By 1819, it was bringing passengers and freight to and from Mackinac Island and other points up the Great Lakes beyond Detroit.

92

Courtesy: Clarke Historical Library

Courtesy: William L. Clements Library

Michigan, in the early years of the nineteenth century, was a remote area. Americans were slow to come to the territory because it was accessible by land or water only after a long and expensive journey. One step toward removing this major impediment to large-scale settlement is illustrated in this 1820 painting of Detroit by George Washington Whistler, gifted father of an even more gifted artist son. Dominating the scene is the *Walk-in-the-Water*, the first steamboat on the Great Lakes above Niagara Falls.

MANIFEST of the whole Boat WALK-IN-THE-WATER— Master; burthen 338 and 60-95ths Mackinac to the Port of **Cargo on board of the Steam-** whereof JOB FISH is at present Tons, bound from the Port of Black Rock June 21st 1819

Marks and Numbers.	No. of Entries.	Packages and Contents.	Shippers.	Residence.	Consignees.	Residence.
J F W	1	Box	Capt Knapp	Mackinac	John F White	Erie
D Deacon	1	Mocock Sugar	D Deacon	On Board	D Deacon	on Board
J H Carr	1	Do Do	J H Carr	do	J H Carr	do
J B Stuart	45	Barrels Fish	J B Stuart	do	J B Stuart	do
D G Jones	18	Hams	D G Jones	do	D G Jones	do
do	1	Pack Furs	do	do	do	do
do	1	Keg	do	do	do	do
do	1	Box Dry Goods	do	do	do	do
do	1	Barrel Do	do	do	do	do
do	4	Boxes Nails	do	do	do	do
L H	4	Barrels Fish	L Hodge	do	do	do
Cheesborough	1	Barrel Fish	Cheesborough	do	do	do
D D	1	Barrel Fish	D Deacon	do	do	do

40 *ARTICLES OF ENTRY.*

DISTRICT OF BUFFALO CREEK, ss.
PORT OF BUFFALO CREEK,

JOB FISH, Master of the Steam-Boat WALK-IN-THE-WATER, having, as the law directs, made oath to the above Manifest consisting of Forty articles of Entry; and delivered a duplicate thereof, permission is hereby granted to the said Master to proceed to the Port of Black Rock in the State of New York Given under my hand and seal of office, at the Custom-House of the Port of Buffalo Creek, the Mackinac, day of this 21 June 1819. and of the Independence of the United States the forty third year,

COLLECTOR.

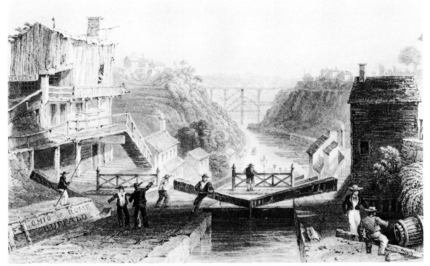

In 1825, the Erie Canal opened, an event that was equally as important to the development of such western areas as Michigan as it was to the economy of New York. The famous canal provided an all-water route connecting New York City and other Eastern markets with Michigan, cutting many days and dollars off the time and the expense that had previously been involved in transporting passengers and goods between these points.

Courtesy: Transportation Library

Later, in its financially disastrous internal improvements program of the late 1830's, Michigan would attempt to build its own canal system across the lower peninsula. Traces of the never-finished Clinton-Kalamazoo Canal which was to have linked Mount Clemens, at the mouth of the Clinton River, with what is now Saugatuck, at the mouth of the Kalamazoo, may still be seen in Macomb and Oakland Counties. This ruined aqueduct near Utica was to have carried canal traffic over the Clinton River.

Courtesy:
Huron-Clinton Metropolitan Authority

At Detroit, as traffic from the East now rapidly increased, facilities were built to take care of the travelers. Woodworth's Steamboat Hotel, opened in 1819, was, until the 1840's, the most famous establishment of its kind in the city; and its proprietor, Uncle Ben Woodworth, was one of Detroit's best-known personalities. The hotel was located on the corner of Woodbridge and Randolph Streets in downtown Detroit.

When settlers began arriving at Detroit, roads were needed over which they could move into the interior of the lower peninsula. The most famous of these was the Chicago Road, which was surveyed in the late 1820's with funds appropriated by Congress. This is a part of a map published in 1825 which showed the surveyed route, with some of the notations made by the surveyors regarding the terrain and other topographical features. Like so many of Michigan's major roads, the Chicago Road's route followed very closely an old Indian trail. The pioneers, however, did not necessarily follow the route as it was surveyed. Since the road was little more than a track worn by the vehicles that passed over it, the drivers of these vehicles did not hesitate to abandon the surveyed route when an easier and shorter path could be found.

Courtesy: Transportation Library

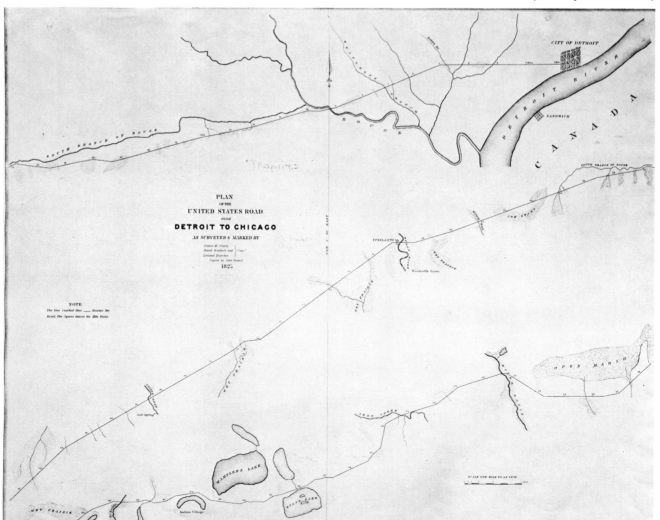

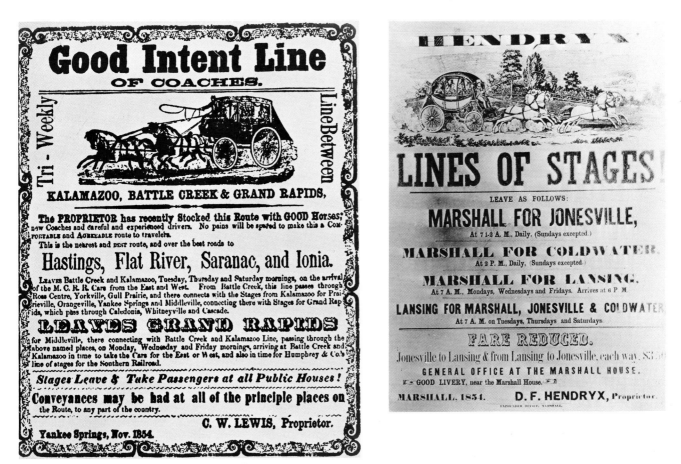

By the 1830's there was regular stagecoach service between Detroit and Chicago over the Chicago Road, and before long, similar service was provided throughout southern Michigan. One of the stages of the Good Intent Line is shown in Plainwell in 1865.

Courtesy: Grand Rapids Public Library

Courtesy: Henry Ford Museum

One of the best-known stagecoach stops along the Chicago Road was this inn at Clinton, built in 1830, which, by the 1920's, had fallen into ruinous condition. At that time, Henry Ford acquired the building and had it removed to the outdoor museum he was developing at Dearborn. Since that time, the Clinton Inn, restored to all of its nineteenth-century majesty, has provided food and relaxation to far more people visiting Ford's Greenfield Village than it ever did during its stagecoach era. The inn is also a fine example of Greek Revival architecture in a commercial structure.

Farther west along the Chicago Road, at Cambridge Junction (the intersection of US-12 and M-50), the old Walker Tavern, built originally in 1832, is another stagecoach stop which has survived and now, after many years of operation as a private historical museum along the lines indicated in this picture, has been purchased by the state to form the nucleus of a historical park.

Another onetime stage stop, the Botsford Inn, located in Farmington on the old Grand River Trail, continues to serve travelers of the modern era as both a restaurant and a hotel. Additions made in the 1950's and 1960's since this photograph was taken have greatly enlarged the original facility, part of which dates from the 1830's.

Courtesy: J. W. Anhut

Not all stagecoach inns were sumptuous affairs, however, as witness this modest establishment, the Robinson Tavern on the Hastings-Battle Creek stage road. Although this tavern was probably more typical of the inns of the day than were the Clinton or Botsford inns, there has been little effort to preserve examples of this type. Here, as elsewhere, the historical preservation movement has always been primarily interested in preserving the superb structures rather than the commonplace.

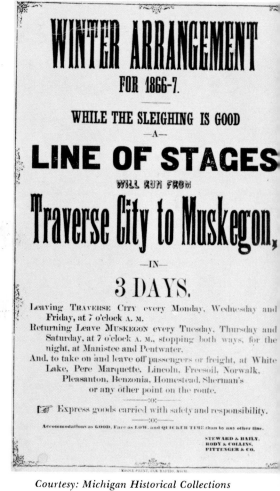

The stagecoach era continued in parts of Michigan until the end of the nineteenth century with special arrangements sometimes made to take advantage of winter road conditions.

In the 1830's the railroad arrived, the final addition to Michigan's nineteenth-century transportation system. Hoping to emulate the success of short-line railroads that developed in the East in the 1820's and early 1830's, many Michigan railroad companies were chartered, although few ever laid a track. The earliest such company to be chartered in Michigan, indeed the first railroad company chartered in the Old Northwest, was the Pontiac and Detroit, whose charter was dated July 31, 1830. The company failed to get anywhere and, in 1834, an entirely new corporation, the Detroit and Pontiac Railroad Company, was organized. Eventually, in 1843, service was actually provided between these two cities. At the Detroit end, travelers could get a room at Hiram R. Andrews' Rail-road Hotel. . . .

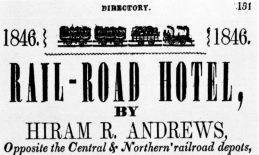

RAIL-ROAD HOTEL,
BY
HIRAM R. ANDREWS,
Opposite the Central & Northern railroad depots,
DETROIT, MICHIGAN,

THIS House has been greatly enlarged and fitted up in a style equal to any Public House in Detroit for comfort and convenience. Its location is one of the most healthy and pleasant in the city,

BEING ON THE PUBLIC SQUARE,

and in the immediate vicinity of the Central and Pontiac Railroad Depots, Auditor General's office, and at the junction of all the leading turnpike roads from Detroit.

GENERAL STAGE OFFICE AT THE HOTEL.

☞ The Proprietor assures the Public that no pains will be spared to furnish his Table with as good as the market affords, and his guests with every attention requisite for their comfort.

TRAVELERS

Wishing to take the Cars or Boats will be
FURNISHED MEALS AT TWENTY-FIVE CENTS,

And Carriage and Baggage Wagon in readiness at all times to convey them to the Cars or Boats, *gratis*.

BOARD BY THE DAY 75 CENTS.

Courtesy: Michigan Historical Collections

. . . A full-page ad in the 1846 Detroit city directory trumpeted some of the services which this hotel offered, including meals "furnished . . . at twenty-five cents" (note the inverted "N's" in the original line!) .

Courtesy: Transportation Library

Michigan's first operating railroad, however, and the first railroad in the West was not the Detroit and Pontiac but the Erie and Kalamazoo, which began running horse-drawn trains between Toledo and Adrian in 1836 and in 1837 started steam operations with a Baldwin locomotive. Just what Michigan's first train looked like is a matter of conjecture. This sketch appeared a half-century after the event, showing the train rolling through the countryside, the pioneers, who were still busily clearing their land, waving at this welcome link with the outside world.

Courtesy: Michigan Historical Collections

A banknote issued by the Erie and Kalamazoo itself is decorated with a picture of a very different-appearing train. It was perhaps not intended to be an exact representation of the Michigan company's rolling stock.

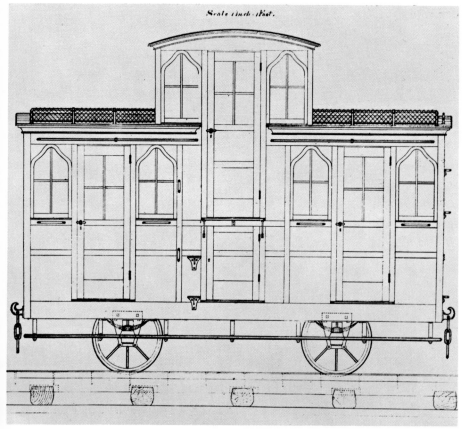

Courtesy: Transportation Library

At any event, this plan for the first Erie and Kalamazoo passenger car does not resemble the cars shown in the two sketches of the railroad's first train.

In the late 1830's railroad lines began to reach across the lower peninsula. By 1838, the Michigan Central offered service from Detroit to Dearborn, and before the year was out its tracks had reached Ypsilanti.

1842.
SEASON ARRANGEMENTS.
MICHIGAN
SOUTHERN RAILROAD,
FROM MONROE TO ADRIAN.

The most direct, expeditious and safest Route.

The public are respectfully notified that the SOUTHERN RAILROAD is now in complete operation *from Monroe to Adrian;* and being well furnished with Locomotives, Passenger and Freight Cars, will transport Freight and Passengers *safer, cheaper and more expeditiously* than any other road in competition.

This road was built by the State of Michigan, at an expense of

Four hundred thousand dollars

and in its construction is not surpassed by any in the United States.

PASSENGERS

Going to Illinois, Indiana, Wisconsin, Iowa and Western, Southern, or Central Parts of Michgian, will perceive, by referring to the Map, that *no Public thoroughfare* is so direct for them as the

SOUTHERN RAILROAD.

☞ *Great care is taken in keeping this Road in good repair, thereby avoiding accidents similar to those occurring upon other roads almost daily, jeopardizing "life and limb."*

STEAMBOATS

Are running from MONROE TO BUFFALO, in connection with the Cars upon this Road.
STAGES, CARRIAGES, WAGONS, ETC.
Are always in attendance to convey Goods and Passengers to any direction from Adrian.
☞ Passengers passing over this Road will be met at the boats by Railroad Cars, and conveyed to the Depot, and from the Depot to the Boats *without charge.*
Cars leave Monroe daily for Adrian, Sundays excepted, at 8 o'clock A. M. and leave Adrian for Monroe at 2 o'clock P. M. Running time 2¼ hours.
The public may rely upon statements here made, and their patronage is respectfully solicited.
J. H. CLEVELAND,
July, 1842.   Superintendent S. R. R.

Rob't. D. Foy, Printer, 159 Main st. Buffalo.

Courtesy: Monroe County Historical Society

By the 1840's more and more communities in southern Michigan were being served by one or more lines. Much of the early impetus came from the state government which began building both the Michigan Central and the Michigan Southern, but in a few years was forced by financial necessity to sell the railroads to private companies, which by the 1850's completed the laying of rails across the state and on to Chicago.

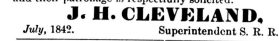

MICHIGAN CENTRAL RAIL-ROAD LINE.

THROUGH IN 34 HOURS IN OPPOSITION TO A VOYAGE FROM 4 1-2 TO 9 DAYS LONG.

OR DETROIT, CHICAGO,

AND OTHER PORTS ON LAKE MICHIGAN.

Courtesy: Transportation Library

Cabin Fare through, (Meals and Berths on Lakes Erie and Michigan included,) $

THROUGH TO DETROIT WITHOUT LANDING!

THROUGH TO CHICAGO IN 34 HOURS—TO MILWAUKEE IN 44 HOURS, AND TO ST. LOUIS IN 3 1-2 DAYS.

By way of MICHIGAN CENTRAL RAILROAD, **518 MILES.**

DISTANCE TO CHICAGO By way of Lakes ST. CLAIR, HURON, AND MICHIGAN. **1056 MILES.**

THE NEW AND SPLENDID STEAMER

ATLANTIC,

CAPT. S. CLEMENT,

Leaves the Michigan Central Railroad Wharf, EVERY MONDAY and THURSDAY EVENING, at NINE O'CLOCK, P. M., in connection with the MICHIGAN CENTRAL RAILROAD, through without landing, arriving at Detroit in time for the Evening Train going West.

From Buffalo to Detroit in 17 Hours. From Detroit to New Buffalo in 11 Hours. From New Buffalo to Chicago in 4 Hours. From Chicago to St. Louis in 48 Hours.

☞ Passengers arriving by the Eastern Cars wishing to take this Boat will please have their Baggage placed under the MICHIGAN CENTRAL RAILROAD SIGN, in the Depot. A Baggaman will be in attendance to convey Baggage to the Boat.

For Passage or Freight, apply on board, or at the Office, at the Michigan Central Railroad Wharf, Buffalo.

Press of Jerome & Brother, Daily American Office, Rochester.

The completion of the Michigan Central between Detroit and Chicago led the railroad company to offer this combination steamboat-train trip linking the East and the West. By taking a steamboat from Buffalo to Detroit, the traveler could then board the Michigan Central, whose depot was located on the Detroit River shore, and proceed to Chicago, thereby cutting several days off the time it took to go from Buffalo to Chicago by boat alone.

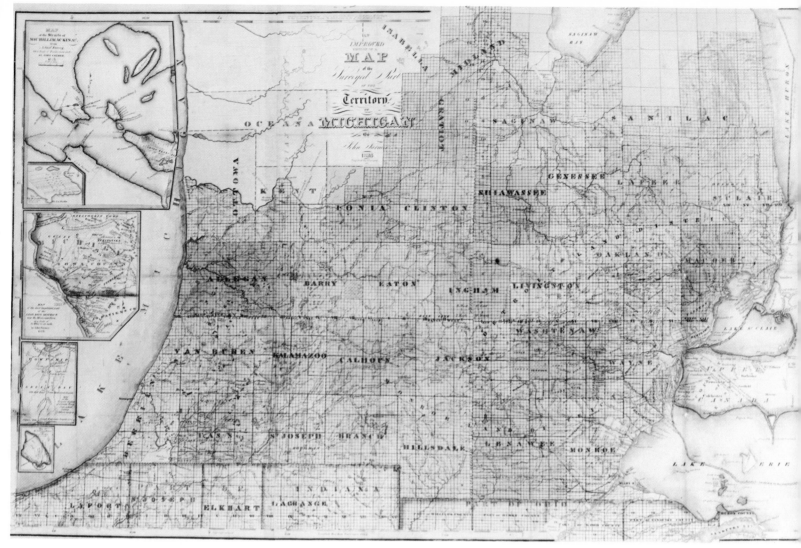

In a matter of but two or three decades, the once remote wilderness had become an easily accessible area to which settlers eagerly flocked. By 1836, John Farmer showed the surveyed parts of Michigan and settlement as stretching clear across the southern third of the lower peninsula from Lake Erie and Lake Huron on the east to Lake Michigan on the west. The advances made since Farmer's first map of 1826 are also shown by the host of new counties that had been created, many of which were named for such prominent officials of the period as Andrew Jackson, Lewis Cass, Martin Van Buren, and John C. Calhoun.

By this time, the population of Michigan Territory was at least one hundred thousand, in contrast with a figure of less than five thousand a quarter of a century earlier. This was far in excess of the population of sixty thousand free inhabitants which had been set by the Northwest Ordinance as the number a territory must contain in order to become a state. Stevens T. Mason, who, as a nineteen-year-old youth, had been named secretary of the territory in 1831, was acting governor much of the time after Cass left in 1831 to become secretary of war. Mason asked Congress to authorize the territory to draw up a state constitution and elect a state government.

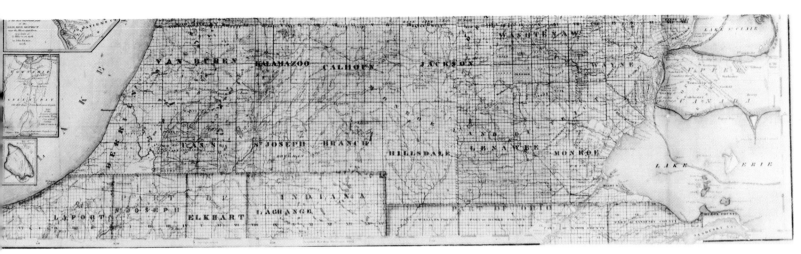

Courtesy: Michigan Historical Collections

Congress refused Mason's request because of a boundary dispute between Ohio and Michigan. Congress in 1787 had declared that the line separating the northern and southern states that would be carved out of the Northwest Territory was to be an east-west line running through the southernmost point of Lake Michigan. This line, as the maps of the period, such as Farmer's map of 1836, clearly showed, intersected Lake Erie some distance south of Miami (Maumee) Bay, placing this area, where the important industrial and port city of Toledo would develop and also a rich band of farm land, in Michigan Territory. Ohio, however, insisted that the Northwest Ordinance line of 1787 had been laid down at a time when no one had realized how far south Lake Michigan extended, and that the direction of the line should be altered in order to give Ohio control of Maumee Bay. Its case was strengthened by the fact that Indiana, as well as Illinois, had successfully pushed their boundaries northward beyond the limits imposed by Congress in 1787. Nevertheless, Michigan insisted that the Toledo strip was rightfully part of its domain. This was the origin of the so-called Toledo War between Michigan and Ohio.

Courtesy: Michigan Department of State

Constitution,

of the

State of Michigan.

In convention, begun at the city of Detroit on the second monday of May, in the year one thousand eight hundred and thirty five.

"We, the PEOPLE of the territory of Michigan, as established by the Act of Congress of the Eleventh day of January, in the year one thousand eight hundred and five, in conformity to the fifth article of the ordinance providing for the government of the territory of the United States North West of the River Ohio, believing that the time has arrived when our present political condition ought to cease, and the right of self-government be asserted; and availing ourselves of that provision of the aforesaid ordinance of the Congress of the United States of the thirteenth day of July, one thousand seven hundred and eighty seven, and the act of congress passed in accordance therewith, which entitle us to admission into the Union, upon a condition which has been fulfilled, do, by our delegates in convention assembled, mutually agree to form ourselves into a free and independent state, by the style and title of "The State of Michigan"; and do ordain and establish the following constitution for the government of the same.

Denied authorization from Congress to proceed with the steps necessary for statehood, acting Governor Mason went ahead on his own. A constitutional convention convened in 1835 and drew up Michigan's first state constitution, a brief document that established a strong central government with few restrictions to hamper the actions of the elected officials, such as would characterize all of Michigan's later constitutions.

103

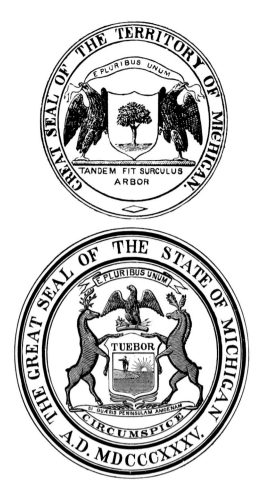

A state seal was adopted by the convention. It was designed by Lewis Cass, who had also designed the seal used by the territorial government since 1814. Its motto, *Tandem fit surculus arbor* ("The shoot at length becomes a tree"), had probably expressed the ultimate desire of Cass to see Michigan grow to statehood. Now, as that goal was being attained, he paraphrased a motto that appears on the tomb of Sir Christopher Wren to point out the unique aspect of the new state: "If you seek a pleasant peninsula, look around you." The word *Tuebor* ("I will defend") was probably intended to indicate Michigan's determination not to give up its claim to the Toledo strip. In the center of the seal, a man is shown holding a gun, standing on a point of land jutting out into the water. The two seals are shown here in their exact original size. The state seal as Cass designed it in 1835 has remained the seal of the state to the present day, although the delineation of the various figures on it has varied considerably over the years, so that today the animals, the eagle, and even the man, bear little resemblance to those shown on the original seal. The great seal can be used on documents or for other purposes only with the permission of the secretary of state. Such permission is not required to use the state coat of arms, which is that material within the outer circles of the seal.

Although Michigan voters late in 1835 approved the state constitution and elected Stevens T. Mason as the first state governor, Congress still would not approve the action and admit Michigan to the union until in 1836 a convention meeting at Ann Arbor in the Washtenaw County Courthouse agreed to surrender the Toledo strip in return for the western two-thirds of the Upper Peninsula. The courthouse in which this historic decision was made was torn down later in the nineteenth century and was replaced by a new building on the same site. The same process was repeated in the middle twentieth century to provide for the present Washtenaw County Courthouse, which will be lucky to survive into the next century.

Courtesy: Michigan Historical Collections

104

CONGRESS OF THE UNITED STATES;

At the *second* Session,

Begun and held at the City of Washington, on Monday, the *fifth* day of December, one thousand eight hundred and *thirty-six*.

AN ACT

to admit the State of Michigan into the Union, upon an equal footing with the original States.

Whereas, in pursuance of the act of Congress of June the fifteenth, eighteen hundred and thirty-six, entitled "An act to establish the northern boundary of the State of Ohio," and to provide for the admission of the State of Michigan into the Union upon the conditions therein expressed," a convention of delegates, elected by the people of the said State of Michigan, for the sole purpose of giving their assent to the boundaries of the said State of Michigan as described, declared, and established, in and by the said act, did, on the fifteenth of December, eighteen hundred and thirty-six, assent to the provisions of said act, therefore: Be it enacted by the Senate and House of Representatives of the United States of America in Congress assembled, That the State of Michigan shall be one, and is hereby declared to be one, of the United States of America, and admitted into the Union on an equal footing with the original States, in all respects whatever. Section 2. And be it further enacted, That the Secretary of the Treasury, in carrying into effect the thirteenth and fourteenth sections of the act of the twenty third of June, eighteen hundred and thirty-six, entitled "An act to regulate the deposites of the public money," shall consider the State of Michigan as being one of the United States.

James K. Polk _____ Speaker of the House of Representatives.

M Van Buren } Vice President of the United States, and President of the Senate.

Approved this 26th January 1837 –

Andrew Jackson

President Andrew Jackson on January 25, 1837, signed the act of Congress which conferred statehood on Michigan. After more than two centuries of colonial status under French, British, and American rule, Michigan had become a self-governing state with a voice in the affairs of the federal union equal to that of the twenty-five other established states.

Courtesy: University of Michigan General Library

In a short time, maps of the new state of Michigan began to appear, such as this one, published in 1838 by T. G. Bradford. Much information was yet needed before the geographical knowledge of Michigan would reach the level it has since attained, but the geographical unit that was called Michigan in 1837 is the same one that exists under this name today. Because of the peculiar shape of the state, which makes it difficult to show the entire area on a normal atlas page, Bradford showed the western half of the Upper Peninsula, in much reduced scale, in an inset, a practice that map makers have commonly used, to the disgust of many residents of those western portions. (Bradford was a little premature in showing the extent of railroad operations in southern Michigan in 1838 and also in showing a canal running from Saginaw to Ionia, which was planned but never completed.)

The famous "war" between Michigan and Ohio fortunately never amounted to much and never reached the stage of real combat and bloodshed. Not until 1915 was the land boundary agreed upon in 1836 officially surveyed. At that time, Governor Woodbridge N. Ferris of Michigan (left) and Governor Frank B. Willis of Ohio shook hands across the state line. The "war," however, is not quite over even yet because the location of the water boundary in Lake Erie is still a matter of dispute between the Wolverine State and the Buckeye State.

Pioneer Architecture

Statehood and self-government were but two of the goals which American pioneers were determined to achieve. The ambitions of the Michigan pioneers are perhaps best exemplified in the buildings which they erected soon after their arrival. Not content with practical, utilitarian structures, they ultimately insisted on importing the best styles they had known in the Eastern states from which they had emigrated. It was appropriate, therefore, that Adrian in 1870 erected as a monument to its Civil War dead a marble Greek Ionic column which had been part of Philadelphia's Bank of Pennsylvania building. Today, this column, the only known fragment from the building with which the architect, Benjamin H. Latrobe, in 1798 had inaugurated the Greek Revival style of architecture in America, stands as a fitting memorial to the pioneers whose building activities adhered to a style which the architectural historian Rexford Newcomb declares "was more exclusively classic than that of any other state of the Old Northwest."

This was Grand Rapids in 1831. In the foreground is the camp of Chief Noonday, a leader of the Ottawa Indians, who still lived in villages along the Grand River and hunted over the surrounding lands, as they and their ancestors had done for centuries. In the background are buildings associated with a Baptist mission, established in 1823, and the fur-trading post of Louis Campau, which he had been operating since 1826.

108

Courtesy: Michigan Historical Collections

Within a few months after the Rev. J. Booth portrayed Grand Rapids as it looked in 1831, Louis Campau, Lucius Lyon, and others who now bought land here began to promote the development of a city and by the time Michigan became a state in 1837, Grand Rapids was a booming community which, its boosters (many of them from western New York) declared, would be the "Rochester of the West." Had photography been sufficiently advanced by this time, the scene in Grand Rapids would probably have been quite similar to this one, taken in May, 1886, in the new Upper Peninsula town of Ironwood, looking west down Aurora Street. The process of pushing back

the frontier was one that did not end in Michigan until the twentieth century, and, in fact, still continues, to some extent, with each new suburban development.

In an amazingly short time, considering the transportation facilities and the construction materials and equipment that were then available, the new towns in Michigan advanced beyond the raw frontier stage. Men of means in these communities were soon moving their families into homes such as this one, built by the Grand Rapids merchant Abraham Pike, in 1844 or 1845, when that city was scarcely a decade removed from being simply an Indian trading and mission settlement.

Courtesy: Allen Stross

109

Although the Pike House, now the home of the Grand Rapids Art Gallery, is in itself an example of how rapidly southern Michigan was transformed from a wilderness into an area of thriving settlements, the great Doric columns that support the central pedimented portico illustrate this movement in an even more startling fashion. They were originally part of a $200,000 hotel built in the 1830's by the promoters of Port Sheldon, a town located on Lake Michigan, some twenty-five miles west of Grand Rapids. Port Sheldon failed to fulfill the dreams of its developers and the town soon disappeared. But the four columns from the hotel, which Abraham Pike bought for the house he was building, epitomize the high ambitions of the Michigan pioneer.

The traditional pioneer dwelling, as every school child knows, was a log cabin, but contrary to what many believe, the Michigan log cabin was not necessarily the typical cabin with walls of round, untrimmed, bark-covered logs. Rather, these cabins, since fur-trading days, were more likely to be constructed of squared logs, as in this abandoned building, located between Lansing and Williamston.

Here was a larger log farm house, again of squared-log construction, which was found in the Houghton Lake area.

This family in the Traverse City area had either begun with, or advanced to, this larger, unpainted frame house, with such luxuries as a stoop outside the entrance for rocking chairs, flower pots, and, hanging from the eaves, a bird cage.

Courtesy: Clarke Historical Library

Courtesy: Historic American Buildings Survey

The examples of nineteenth-century houses which are carefully preserved and pointed out to visitors who want to see old buildings, however, are not the average residential buildings of the period, few of which have survived, but the exceptional and very fine architectural examples, especially the Greek Revival house. The best known, certainly the most frequently mentioned and pictured, is the Harold Brooks House, on the corner of North Kalamazoo Avenue and Prospect Street in Marshall. With its great two-story portico of five fluted Ionic columns, its carved ornamental window in the pediment above the columns, . . .

. . . its entrance through a one-story Ionic porch on one side, its interior decoration (we overlook the jarring note of the mid-1930's furnishings) , this brick house is a magnificent structure, built by Jabez S. Fitch around 1840, scarcely a decade after Marshall was founded.

Courtesy: Historic American Buildings Survey

The Brooks House is by no means unique. Numerous other superb examples of Greek Revival architecture abound in southern Michigan, including such other examples of the two-story, temple-style mansion as the Wilson-Wahr House at 126 North Division Street, Ann Arbor, built in 1843. Its location on a smaller corner lot does not set off the house to such an advantage as do the more extensive grounds of the Harold Brooks House, but the Wilson-Wahr House is considered by Rexford Newcomb to be "one of the finest Greek Revival houses in America." Great full-length windows beneath the portico look out from the parlor.

114

Courtesy: Historic American Buildings Survey

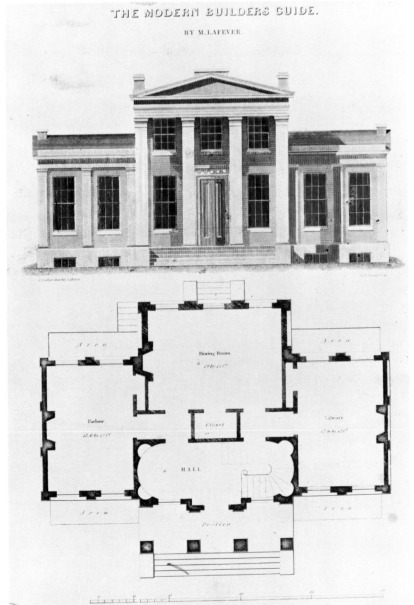

There were innumerable variations of the Greek Revival style. Somewhat similar to the Pike House in Grand Rapids is the Sidney T. Smith House on Michigan Road, just west of Maute Road, in the vicinity of Grass Lake. The house, built in 1840, has a two-story central section, flanked by one-story wings, all fronted by square-columned porticoes. It appears that Smith, like modern home builders who pore over books of model homes to get ideas, patterned his house after a model for a country villa in Minard Lafever's *Modern Builder's Guide,* first published in 1833.

Courtesy: University of Michigan Architectural Library

Not all Greek Revival houses present
a massive appearance. An early and
unusual type is the Elijah Anderson
House, West Chicago Boulevard at
North Union Street, Tecumseh, built
in 1832. Some of its features,
such as the dormer, were added at a
later date and serve to detract
from the original classic design.

Courtesy: Historic American Buildings Survey

Courtesy: Historic American Buildings Survey

A house does not have to have an imposing,
multi-columned portico to qualify as a
Greek Revival building, as witness the
Sibley House at 976 East Jefferson Avenue,
Detroit, which was built by the political
leader Solomon Sibley in the 1840's. It
is now the rectory of Christ (Episcopal)
Church.

Although the Greek Revival style was the dominant
one for many years in the homes built by
successful Michiganians, other types were not
unknown. Traits of the earlier Federal style were
evident in the John Palmer House in Detroit, which
was built in 1829 and torn down four decades later.

116

Courtesy: Allen Stross

Somewhat later came such modifications of the Greek Revival style as the bracketed Italianate style, exemplified by the Chauncey M. Brewer mansion at 410 North Eagle Street, Marshall, which was completed in 1859.

Courtesy: Grand Rapids Public Library

Then there were the unusual types, such as the octagon houses, whose supposed virtues were advocated by the eccentric phrenologist Orson A. Fowler. He found a number of converts to his ideas in mid-nineteenth-century Michigan, from which period dates the Ira Jones cobblestone octagon house at 706 Butterworth Street, Grand Rapids.

The one-story brick octagon house at 1520 Long Road, Kalamazoo, now owned by Mrs. J. Stanley Gilmore, shows the eight-sided form of the main mass of the building carried through in the cupola which lights the central interior.

Courtesy: Kalamazoo Gazette

Courtesy: Allen Stross

In a class by itself is the Honolulu House, located at 107 North Kalamazoo Avenue, in that city of well-preserved old houses, Marshall. Abner Pratt built this house in 1860, supposedly using as his model a house which he had occupied while serving as United States consul to Hawaii. Both in its exterior appearance and in its ornate interior decoration, the Honolulu House, now maintained as a historic house museum, has been hailed by the architectural historian Harley J. McKee as "a unique and highly interesting piece of architecture and decoration."

Courtesy: Michigan Historical Collections

Michigan is fortunate to have so many well-preserved residential houses from this great architectural era. Many more, like this neglected, rundown country home in Livingston County, have disappeared or are gradually falling into a state virtually beyond repair.

Politics and Government

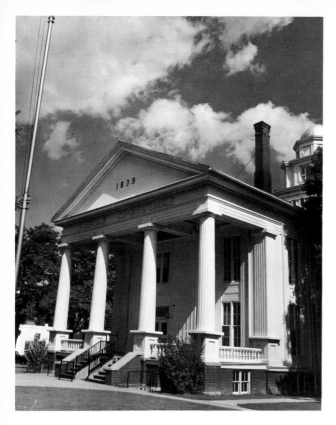

As the date inscribed on the pediment indicates, the Lapeer County Courthouse in Lapeer was erected in the midst of the period when classic models were the fashion among Michigan's builders and architects. The degree of attrition that has taken place among Michigan's public buildings dating from the pioneer period, however, has been far higher than that which has occurred among the private residences built at that time. For many years the Lapeer County Courthouse has held the distinction of being Michigan's oldest courthouse, but it has been in constant danger from those who have wanted to replace it with a larger, more efficient, modern structure.

It must be admitted, however, that the pioneers were often much more conservative in providing adequate housing for their government offices than they were for themselves. The first Ingham County Courthouse in Mason was built in 1843 at a cost which the county supervisors directed must not exceed $800. Within a few years the need for larger quarters for the county officials led to the construction of a new courthouse, this time at an expense of $12,229.19. Completed in 1858, the new building, designed by Matthew Elder of Lansing, was a more imposing structure, but it barely survived into the twentieth century before it, too, was replaced.

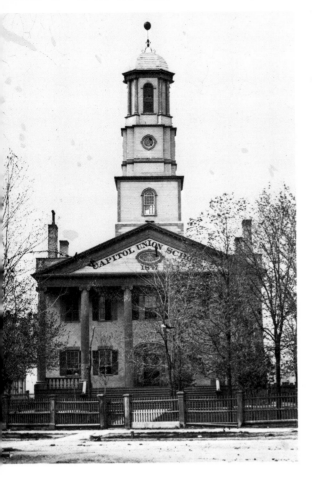

Courtesy: Burton Historical Collection

So far as the government of Michigan was concerned, the story was somewhat reversed. In the 1820's, the territorial government moved into what was for the time an impressive and commodious brick capitol, after having met in various temporary quarters since the establishment of the territory in 1805. The new capitol, which later, until it burned in 1893, was used by Detroit as a school building, cost $21,000 and was one of the earliest Greek Revival buildings in Michigan, with a fine Ionic portico and a tower which rose to a height of 140 feet.

In 1847, ten years after Michigan officially became a state, the state constitution required that a decision be made as to where the capital of Michigan should be permanently located. Communities throughout southern Michigan contested with Detroit, which had been the temporary capital, for the honor, with the Legislature finally choosing a wilderness site in central Michigan which would later be named Lansing. Here, by the next session of the Legislature in January, 1848, a plain, quietly modest frame capitol was built at an original cost that was considerably less than the cost of the first Michigan capitol building in the 1820's. Economy-minded legislators knew at the time that the new capitol would be totally inadequate for the needs of the state in a few years, but not enough of them were willing to risk their careers by supporting the appropriations that would have been required to build a structure of more realistic dimensions.

The only state building in Lansing from this early period that still survives is this house, which the Legislature, with a wisdom it has not shown since, had built in 1850 as the official residence for the governor. The state's chief executives, however, refused to use the house, declaring that it did not meet the requirements necessary for such an important office. For a time, other state officials lived in the house, which stood at the corner of Allegan and Capitol in downtown Lansing. Later, in the twentieth century, after the house had been sold to a private individual, it was moved far out to what were then the outskirts of town at 2003 West Main, where the house is still used as a private residence.

Towering over Michigan's political and governmental affairs throughout these years, as few men since have done, was Lewis Cass, still a very active figure when he sat before the camera in the 1850's. Cass did not need to caution the photographer, as he had some earlier portrait painters, not to hide any warts or wrinkles. The daguerreotype taken that day was brutally frank in the image it left of an old statesman, now in his seventies, tired and disillusioned from the strains and conflicts and frustrations of half a century of unending political life. He had been governor of Michigan Territory, secretary of war in Andrew Jackson's cabinet, minister to France, and United States senator from Michigan. Ahead of him lay one of his most important jobs, that of secretary of state under President James Buchanan, but he knew that his ultimate dream, that of becoming President of the United States, was now a thing of the past, something that he could now no longer hope to achieve.

From an earlier period in his life is this rather ridiculous portrait of Cass in which he is shown with a Roman toga thrown over his nineteenth-century dress. Such a pose, which reflected the same obsession with classical models that spawned the Greek Revival fad, had been popular in paintings and statues of the founding fathers of the republic, in whose footsteps Cass, like any other ambitious politician of his day, sought to follow.

THE PRESIDENTIAL FISHING PARTY OF 1848.

THE STRIFE between an old HUNKER a BARNBURNER and a NO PARTY MAN.

Cass came very close to becoming President in 1848 when he was nominated for the office by the Democratic Party, the only resident of Michigan to be so honored by a major party. (Thomas E. Dewey, who was born in Owosso, had long since become a New York resident when he was the two-time Republican presidential candidate a century later.) As these cartoons suggest, however, in the labored style typical of the era, Cass had to contend not only with the other major party candidate, the military hero Zachary Taylor, but also with a formidable nominee of the Free-Soil Party, former President Martin Van Buren. Van Buren's opposition to slavery won him enough votes among antislavery Democrats in New York to prevent Cass, whose stand on slavery did not please the ardent foes of that institution, from winning that state's electoral votes. This in turn was enough to give Taylor the majority he needed to win and therefore deny Cass the office for which he had been preparing throughout his adult years.

Lewis Cass was one reason why the Democrats were the dominant party in Michigan from the time that elections were first held in the territory in the 1820's until the decade of the fifties. In the first election after Michigan became a state in 1837, the hero of Michigan's struggle to achieve statehood, Stevens T. Mason, was returned to the governor's office by an overwhelming Democratic majority. The painter T. H. O. P. Burnham depicted the scene in Detroit on election day in a somewhat Hogarthian manner. Mason is shown left center in a tall black hat, with a cigar in his mouth, caught in the act, some think, of buying votes. Nearby, two drunks seem to be standing in line for their payment, while over on the right a heated discussion on the merits of the candidates is underway and a Mason supporter seated on horseback holds aloft a Democratic banner. In the background, a procession of Whig Party people, one carrying a banner that states, "Provisions for the poor if the Whigs carry the day," advances from the left toward city hall, into which a ballot box is being carried.

DETROIT GAZETTE.

VOL. I. DETROIT, MICHIGAN TERRITORY, FRIDAY, JULY 25, 1817. NO. 1

PUBLISHED BY
SHELDON & REED,
In Attwater-st. a few rods above the Public Wharf.

TERMS.

This paper will be afforded to city subscribers and those in the vicinity at $4 per annum:

To subscribers who receive their papers by mail, at $3 50 per ann. payable in advance:

To classes often or more, who take their papers at the office, 5 cents per paper.

Advertisements will be inserted for $1 50 per square for the first three insertions, and 37 1-2 cents for each continuation.

BOOKS.

SHELDON & REED have just opened and offer for sale, at the office of the GAZETTE, a good collection of Books, among which are the following:

Quarto, octavo and School Bibles; Nouveau Testament, Dufief's Nature Displayed, Flint's Survey, Shey's Bookkeeping, Jacksons do. Walker's, Perry's, Entick's and Johnson's Dictionary, Scottish Chiefs, Montgomery's Poems, the Wreath Vicar of Wakefield, Volney's Ruins, Thaddeus of Warsaw, Thinks-I-to-Myself, Songster's Companion, Thompson's Seasons, Junius, Memoirs of Washington, Lady of the Lake, Life of Trenck, Goldsmith's Poems, Farmer's Boy, Campbell's Poems, Terrible Tractoration! Blair's Lectures, Perrin's French Fables, Bennett's Letters, Works of Lord Byron, Shipwreck, Goldsmith's history of Greece, Rome and England, Don Quixotte, Cowper's Works, Bigland's Letters on History, Beauties of Poetry, Fool of Quality, Freemason's Monitor, Velvet Cushion, Life of Franklin, Rollin's Ancient History Indian Wars, Morse's Universal Geography and Atlas, Morse's Gazetteer, Chateaubriand's Travels, Peregrine Pickle, Twin Sisters, Life of Lay and Sandiford, Gazetter of Upper Canada, with and without Maps, Musical Miscellany, &c. Also

STATIONARY,

Ledgers, Journals, Day Books, Paper, Quills, Ink Powder, black and red Sealing wax, wafers, Inkstands, Reeves' water colors and camel's hair pencils, India Ink and rubber, pocket books, office seals, and almost every other article in the stationary line.

SCHOOL BOOKS.

in a great variety—Children's Books.
Detroit, July 25, 1817.

GLOBE TAVERN.

THE Subscriber begs leave to inform the citizens and inhabitants of the city of Detroit and territory of Michigan, that he has commenced the business of Tavernkeeping, at the sign of the Golden Ball, in said city. From the local situation of his house, and the unremitted attention which will be paid those who may honor him with their custom, he anticipates a generous patronage from the community. Gentlemen visiting this country from the eastern and southern states, he also hopes, will do him the honor to call on him.—OLIVER WILLIAMS.
Detroit, July 21, 1817.

LARNED & WATSON,

[*Opposite the Market.*]
Have for sale, a general assortment of

Dry Goods, Groceries, and Hardware.

—ALSO—
30 Barrels WHISKEY,
50 do. FLOUR;
20 do. Rectified and common SALT;
Empty Pipes, Hogsheads and Barrels.
Detroit, July 23, 1817. 1tf

LAND OFFICE. Detroit July 19, 1817

Public Notice

IS hereby given to all those inhabitants, owning, or claiming lands, lying, situate, and not extending in depth to eighty arpents, French measure, that in pursuance of an act of Congress, passed the 3d of March, 1817, the United States' Land Office, for the district of Detroit, will be opened at the Council-House in the city of Detroit, on the first Thursday in August, at ten o'clock in the forenoon, when the Commissioners will attend to receive and adjust such claims as may be filed with the Register of the said Land Office, at Detroit, according to the second section of the said act.
PETER AUDRAIN, *Register.*

27 Barrels of Wahatomaka *WHISKEY;*

Just landed from the schr. Merchant (WING's Wharf)—For sale on very reasonable terms, by
JNO. STOCKTON.
July 18th, 1817. 1tf

New Wholesale and Retail

STORE.

H. PEIRCE & CO.

Have just opened a Store at the *Rivre Raisin*, where they offer for sale a well chosen assortment of

DRY GOODS;

Among which are

FINE and coarse BROADCLOTHS,
Cashmeres, Webbs Velvets,
Dressed and undressed Calicoes,
Furniture do.
Red, yellow black and green Flannels from 30 cents to $1.50 per yard.
Bombazetts, Ratimetts, Bombazines,
Silks, Lustings,
Levantines, Florentines,
Silk Shawls and Handkerchiefs,
Cambricks, Dimites,
Sarsenett, Figured, Mull, Plain, Tambour'd India and Book Muslins,
Lenoes, Janes, Ginghams,
100 Pieces elegant assorted Ribbons,
Lace Veils, black and white,
Ladies' Plumes, Artificial Flowers,
Cheneid Cords of various colors,
Men's and Women's Cotton Hose,
do do Silk do. white & black,
Assorted Worsted do.
Gloves of almost every description,
Crape, Tambor'd Trimmings,
Sewing Silks, Galloons,
Quality and Shoe Binding,
Linen and Cotton Threads,
Cotton Ferrets, Buttons,
Umbrellas, Tapes, Pins, &c. &c.
A large assortment of Men's and Women's SHOES;
A good supply of INDIAN GOODS—*Traders* will do well by calling.

.....

GROCERIES.

COGNIAC BRANDY, 4th proof;
Cider do.
Jamaica and St. Croix SPIRITS;
GIN; good WHISKEY;
Madeira and Port WINES;
Imperial, Young Hyson, } TEAS.
Hyson Skin & Souchong }
SUGARS; Pepper; Allspice;
TOBACCO, Segars, &c. &c.

—ALSO—

Hardware, Crockery,
AND
AMERICAN GOODS
of every description.

N.B.—The above Goods will be sold as low as any in the Michigan Territory. Considerable deduction will be made to Wholesale Purchasers—FURS received in payment.
River Raisin, July 25, 1817. 1tf

D. C. M'KINSTRY

Has received—ON CONSIGNMENT;
FORTY bbls. Rectified WHISKEY;
10 do. Prime PORK;
9 do. LARD;
3 do. OIL (Linseed.)
80 Mococks of SUGAR;
6 doz. Castor and Roram HATS.
—ALSO—
1000 pieces of Domestic Earthern Ware;
40 Tons of handsome building Stone, from Cleveland; and
A general assortment of TIN WARE.

Any orders for Earthern or Tin Ware can be answered on a short notice, from the Factories at Grand River, in the state of Ohio.

ALSO, FOR SALE,
100 pair of Nankeen Pantaloons and Roundabouts, and a general assortment of READY MADE CLOTHING.

A small assortment of

DRY GOODS;

Together with the following articles of GROCERIES:

Whiskey and Jamaica Rum,
[by the Gallon.]
PEPPER, | ALLSPICE,
GINGER, | TOBACCO, &c.

The above Goods will be sold very low for ready pay.

N.B. 10 Bbls. good CIDAR VINEGAR for sale.
30,000 Pine SHINGLES;
15,000 Hemlock LATH.
Detroit, July 25, 1817.

Drugs and *Medicines.*

THE subscriber takes this method to inform the Public that he has opened a small but good assortment of DRUGS and MEDICINES, which he offers for sale at a very moderate advance.

N. B.—He will punctually attend to any calls with which he may be honored, either in the practice of Medicine or Surgery.
JOHN L. WHITING.
Detroit, July 24th, 1817. 1tf

PUBLIC NOTICE

IS HEREBY GIVEN, That Proposals will be received by the Governor and Judges, at the Council House, on Monday the fourth day of August next, at 11 o'clock A. M. for the following materials and work for a Stone Jail.

1st. 250 toises of stone, from Stony Island, one half of which is to be delivered on the interior of section number 7 by the first day of December next, and the residue by the middle of June next.

The number of toises is to be ascertained by the actual measurement of the walls when the building is completed; but the contractor will be paid by estimate when one third, when two thirds, and when the whole of the stone is delivered; but so much of the price will be retained as to render it certain that the amount paid shall not at the measurement exceed the value of the stone delivered. Should a greater quantity than 250 toises be found necessary to complete the Jail, the contractor will be obligated to deliver them at the same rate upon the requisition of the superintendent.

2d. As many barrels of stone lime as may be necessary to complete the building, to be delivered at the same place, one hundred barrels by the middle of May next, and the residue as it may be required by the superintendent of the building.

3d. As much of the best river sand and as much water as may be necessary for the work; the former to be delivered as may be required by the said superintendent, and the latter from day to day as the progress of the work may require.

4th. The Mason's work upon the said Jail agreeably to a plan and description to be seen at the office of the subscriber.

The whole to be completed on or before the first day of October, 1818; and the contractor to find everything necessary, except the stone, lime, sand and water.

5th. The Carpenter's and Joiners work upon the said building, agreeably to the above mentioned plan and description.

The whole to be completed by the first day of December, 1818, and the contractor to find everything which may be necessary, except the glass, nails, paint and iron work.

6th. The glass, nails, paint and iron work for the said building, to be furnished agreeably to the plan and the requisition of the Superintendent.

The materials and workmanship are to be of the best kind, and the whole to be approved by and to be under the direction of the Superintendent.

The Contracts are to be separate, and good security for the performance will be required. AUSTIN E. WING.
Secretary.
Detroit, July 25, 1817.

B. STEAD—Taylor, &c.

TAKES the opportunity of the first commencement of a Newspaper in Detroit, to express his gratitude to the citizens thereof for their liberal patronage, and assures them that no exertion shall be omitted on his part, to continue to deserve it.

Officers of the Army and gentlemen whose remote situation may make it convenient to them to give orders personally, by sending their order and dimensions, (as under) may depend upon being furnished without delay with any article, *warranted* of the best materials, fashion, and workmanship.

	Feet.	*Inches.*
Height - - - - -		
Thickness round the breast		
Thickness round the waist		
Top of the arm - -		
Top of the thigh - -		
Under the knee cap - -		
Calf - - - -		

N. B.—Those Ladies who may honor B. S. with their commands, for Habits, Pelisses, or Riding Coats, by sending their height and thickness round the breast and waist, shall at all times meet with immediate attention.
Detroit, July 25, 1817. 1tf

DETROIT HAT FACTORY.

PAUL CLAP,

RESPECTFULLY informs the inhabitants of Detroit and its vicinity, that he has on hand, and will constantly keep at his Factory, two doors east of the sign of the *Golden Ball*, a large and good assortment of

Beaver,
Castor,
Roram, } *HATS,*
Knapt &
Felt,

For sale, WHOLESALE and RETAIL.
**CASH paid for FURS.
July 27th, 1817. 1tf

SPELLING BOOKS by the doz. at this office.

J. M'DONELL.

HAS on hand, for Sale at his Store, the following articles: viz.

DRY GOODS.

BROADCLOTHS, Sattinetts,
Yellow white, and red Flannel,
Green Baize, Bed Ticking, Cotton Checks,
Striped Genet, white do. Princes Cord,
Fine white Marseilles, printed do.
Black silk Florentine, Book Muslin,
Muslinett, Jaconett, Cambrick,
Princes stripe, twilled, sattin striped Jaconet,
Japan Muslin, Lawn striped, Lappet do.
Cluster mull'd, cambric Muslin,
Buff striped Gingham, cambric do.
Silk Plaid, corded do. plaid Cambrick,
Colored cambrick, striped do. slate do.
Furniture calico, Bombazines,
Black mode, Green Florence,
Black Lustring, Canton crape, Long Lawn,
Cotton Lace, Vandyke do. black do.
Velvet Ribbon, black Bombazette,
Green Wildboar, Pocket handkerchiefs,
Figured Madrass, blue do.
Flag handkerchiefs, cotton do.
Cotton blue Bandannas, red do. Turkey twil'd
Black Canton handkerc'fs, elegant white lace
Shawls, Black do. black lace Veils,
Black silk Hose, ladies white do. do.
White habit silk Gloves, long do. gentlemen's beaver do. ladies' kid do.
Suspenders, bobbins, tapes, black sewing s'lk
Nankeen do. fancy do. twist, white threads of all numbers, colored threads,
Common Fans, fancy do. tipp'd with ivory,
Shirt buttons, lace do. cotton balls, col'd do.
Silk Purses, a variety of Ribbons, Taste,
Sattins, Galoons, head ornaments,
Artificial Flowers, Parasols, &c. &c.

Hardware.

Hambro lines, cod do. clothes do. bed cords, hoe hammers, screw augers, steelyards, G. S. hand and pannel saws, iron post coffee mills, ink, powder, (black and red) shaving boxes, H L hinges, H do. chest do. round bolts, rivet gimlets, stock locks, fine s. bitted, chafing dishes, wire mouse traps, wood do, single pad locks, double do. covered cupboard locks, bolt knob do. awl hafts, thumb latches, Norfolk do. C. S. sickels, snaffles, spoon end bitts do. chalk lines, fish do. blacking, Britannia tea spoons, table do. silver, plaited do. silver plaited tea do. brass cocks, shoe pincers, japan tobacco boxes, polished steel do. Fermer's chissels, gouge do. fluting do. pod augers, slates, shaving soap, rag stones, pocket glasses, sheep shears, carpenter's rules, saddler's webb, screws of all sizes, clothes brushes, awl blades, tooth brushes, shoe knives, pocket books, quills, flat files, C. S. b's'd. do. shoe rasps, pocket inkstands, pocket compasses, bellows, razor strops, japan lamps, candlesticks, (common and plated), paper snuff boxes, thimbles of various kinds, japanned inlets, carpenter's compasses, Flemish tacks, inkstands, heel ball, key hole saws, fancy dressing cases complete, snuffer trays, lead pencils, slate pencils, single and double temple spectacles, green do. smoothing irons, English Brooms, Dutch do. scrubbing brushes, paint do. shoe do. hearth do. shovels, spades, frying pans, razors, scissors, combs, barlow knives, pen knives of various descriptions, pocket do. pruning do. knives and forks of different descriptions, table steels, hand-saw files, cut saw do. Waters' best grass scythes, plated bitts, bardoons and curbs, ivory combs, plated snaffle bitts, plated stirrups, fish hooks, plated hooks & eyes, back gammon tables, W. C. needles, darning do. sail do. pencil cases, gilt watch chains, ear rings, broaches, ladies' pocket books, watch glasses, composition tea kettles, womens' combs, side do. sun glasses, tin scales, a variety of small looking glasses, Powder and shot, &c.

An assortment of

Crockery Ware,

Stationary.

Spelling books of various kinds, chap books, toy books, black and red sealing wax, playing cards, steel ring purses, Reeves colors, blank books, a variety of novels.

Drugs and Medicines.

Rawson's itch ointment, Turlington's Balsam, Essence of pepper mint, castor oil, Church's cough drops, Lee's pills, Anderson's do. Magnesia, arrow root, pomatum, spece bottles with covers, essence of Lavender, Burgamot, Camphor, Godfrey's cordial, Chentz's Worm Lozenges, Opodeldoc, Solomon's celebrated BALM OF GILEAD, Stoughton's Bitters, tooth ache drops, liquorice ball, tooth powder, Bark pulv. rub. Glauber salts, refined.

Groceries.

Cogniac BRANDY;
Sicily Madeira, }
Port, }
Colemaner. } WINES.
L. P. Teneriffe, }
Sherry, }
Hyson Skin, }
Young Hyson, } TEAS.
Hyson, }
Imperial, }

Coffee, Loaf Sugar, Muscovado do. best Spanish Segars, Pepper, Logwood, sweet Oil, spirits of turpentine, Chocolate, dry citron, pearl barrice, capers, olives, tobacco, mustard, almonds, raisins, cloves, nutmegs, cassia, ginger, snuff, tamarinds, black lead, ivory black, lamp black, lime juice, and a great variety of other articles too tedious to mention—all of which will be sold low for cash. DETROIT, July 25, 1817.

Courtesy: Burton Historical Collection

Two of the figures in Burnham's painting hold copies of Detroit newspapers, which is certainly no accident in this political panorama. In that period, newspapers were identified far more definitely than in modern times with a particular political party or faction. Many papers survived as long as they did simply because they were a necessary organ. The Detroit *Gazette*, the second newspaper to be published in Michigan and the first to continue to appear over an extended period of time, was, from its founding in 1817 until its demise in 1830, a Democratic paper.

Courtesy: Burton Historical Collection

The need for a Democratic Party paper to take the place of the Detroit *Gazette* led to the appearance on May 5, 1831, of the first issue of the Detroit *Democratic Free Press and Michigan Intelligencer,* which continues today as the Detroit *Free Press,* Michigan's oldest newspaper. The *Free Press,* which remained a staunch supporter of the Democrats until the end of the nineteenth century, in the fall of 1835 became the first Michigan paper to be issued on a daily basis.

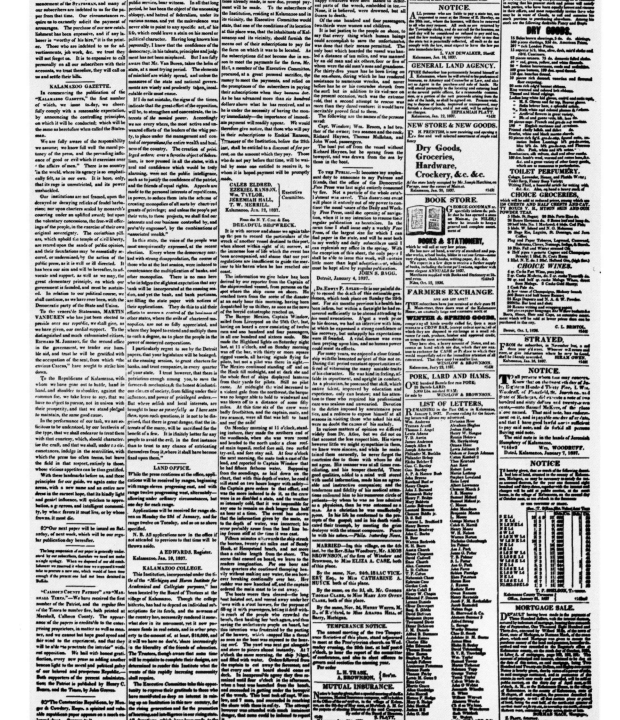

The second oldest paper in Michigan published under the same name down to the present is the Kalamazoo *Gazette,* which originated in 1833 as the *Michigan Statesman and St. Joseph Chronicle* and was published in White Pigeon. Shortly after the United States land office at White Pigeon was moved to Kalamazoo, the newspaper was moved to that city also. Beginning on January 23, 1837, the paper began to appear under the title of Kalamazoo *Gazette.*

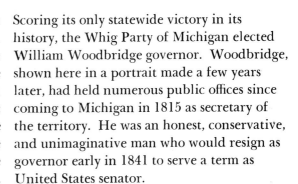

The good times that contributed to the success of Governor Mason and the Democrats were soon forgotten in the late 1830's, when a severe depression hit the nation. The new state government found itself in serious financial troubles which were blamed on the Democratic administration. The Whig Party took advantage of the opportunity in 1839 to throw out "the office-holding tories," as the Democrats were described in this campaign poster.

Scoring its only statewide victory in its history, the Whig Party of Michigan elected William Woodbridge governor. Woodbridge, shown here in a portrait made a few years later, had held numerous public offices since coming to Michigan in 1815 as secretary of the territory. He was an honest, conservative, and unimaginative man who would resign as governor early in 1841 to serve a term as United States senator.

Stevens T. Mason's career, which had begun so brilliantly, ended tragically in 1843 when he died at the age of thirty-one in New York City. He had gone to New York shortly after completing his second term as governor, his reputation and popularity in Michigan greatly diminished by the difficulties which, in modern terminology, had given the young state a poor image. Early in the twentieth century, Mason's remains were brought to Michigan and buried on the old capitol grounds in Detroit and a statue erected to honor belatedly the man who had successfully led Michigan into the union.

127

In 1841, the Democrats turned to an outstate man, John S. Barry, to return to power. Barry made frugality in government his watchword and thereby succeeded in becoming Michigan's only three-term governor in the nineteenth century. His home in Constantine, built about 1840, is still preserved.

Courtesy: Michigan Historical Collections

Courtesy:

University Archives, Western Michigan University

Robert McClelland (left) of Monroe and Detroit, who served as governor, represented Michigan in Congress, and was secretary of the interior under President Franklin Pierce; Alpheus Felch (center) of Ann Arbor, who, at one time or another in a long career, held the offices of governor, United States senator, and state Supreme Court justice, along with miscellaneous other positions; and Charles Stuart (right) of Kalamazoo, who was one of the leading Democratic United States senators in the 1850's—these were some of the most important Michigan Democrats in this era of Democratic ascendancy. The list of offices they held is more impressive than the list of their accomplishments in office, which perhaps explains why their names are now generally forgotten.

128

By the 1850's the question of slavery forced all others to the background, bringing about a fundamental realignment of Michigan's political factions. Opponents of slavery had been active in Michigan for many years, with women emerging for the first time in Michigan as major leaders in such a movement. Elizabeth Margaret Chandler, whose talents as a poet are symbolized in this portrait by the pen she holds in her hand, was already, when she came to Lenawee County in 1830 from the East, one of the better-known figures in the antislavery movement, although she was only twenty-three years old. Like so many of her fellow Quakers in the Lenawee County area and elsewhere, she opposed slavery on moral grounds. In 1832, Miss Chandler took the initiative in the organization of the Michigan Antislavery Society. Elizabeth Chandler died in 1834, but the antislavery work she had begun was carried on by others.

Courtesy: Michigan Historical Collections

Through the efforts of Miss Chandler, another Lenawee County Quaker, Laura Smith Haviland, became interested in the fight against slavery. Mrs. Haviland spent most of her remaining years before, during, and after the Civil War working to free the Negro and at the Raisin Institute, which she and her husband founded, to provide the training and other assistance that the Negro would need when he gained his freedom.

Courtesy: Burton Historical Collection

Sojourner Truth, a Negro who had been born a slave in New York early in the nineteenth century and who was subsequently freed, came to Michigan in the 1850's and made her home in Battle Creek. Long active in the abolitionist movement as an untrained but effective speaker and singer at meetings, she continued her work from Battle Creek until her death in 1883, leaving behind a record in which fact had become so mixed with legend that biographers have unraveled her life's story only with great difficulty.

Michigan residents sheltered fugitive slaves who escaped from the South and fled to the North. In later years, an amazingly large number of people would claim to have been engaged in this illegal activity, the penalties for which, if caught and convicted, became especially severe in the 1850's. There is scarcely a town in southern Michigan which does not have one or more buildings which the local residents will swear was a "station" on the Underground Railroad. This house in Union City is apparently one whose claim is more authentic than that of some others.

This marker in Marshall locates the site of the cabin which an escaped slave from Kentucky, Adam Crosswhite, and his family, occupied in 1847 when several Kentuckians, including Crosswhite's owner, arrived to take the family back South. The citizens of Marshall forcibly prevented the Kentuckians from carrying out their mission, although the Southerners had the law on their side. The Crosswhites were spirited away to final safety in Canada, and the Crosswhite Case became one of the legal battles over the return of fugitive slaves that served to divide the North and the South.

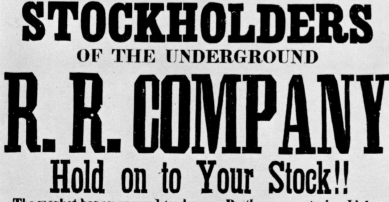

Detroit was the last stop on the road to freedom for the fugitive. This was a handbill distributed in Detroit in 1853, openly proclaiming the successful passage of twenty-nine slaves across to the Canadian side of the Detroit River and calling for donations to help the escapees establish themselves as farmers.

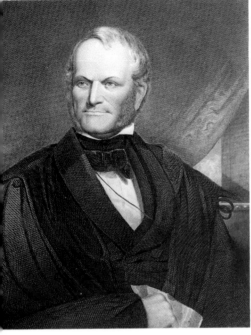

Courtesy: Michigan Historical Collections

Slavery as a political issue had been agitated in the 1840's by the ex-Alabama slaveholder James G. Birney, who settled in Bay City in 1841, the year after he ran for President on the Liberty Party ticket. Birney ran for governor in 1843, and for President again in 1844, and although the votes he received were relatively few, he paved the way for the subsequent Free-Soil Party, which torpedoed the presidential ambitions of Lewis Cass, and finally the Republican Party, on whose ticket Birney's son James would be elected lieutenant governor in 1860.

In 1854, a new party sprang up throughout the North as a result of the Kansas-Nebraska Act, which opened to the slaveholder territories in the West which the farmers of Michigan and other states in the Old Northwest had looked upon as future homesites for themselves and their sons. At Jackson, Michigan, on July 6, a convention of men opposed to the act met "Under the Oaks" because no hall was large enough to accommodate all of the delegates. Here the term "Republican" was first applied to the nascent party. This is the origin of Jackson's claim to being the birthplace of the Republican Party, a claim that received considerable support in 1910 when President William Howard Taft took part in a parade, his car preceded by the famous Jackson Zouave Drill Team, as part of a great civic celebration that was climaxed by the dedication of a bronze plaque at Second and West Franklin Streets which proclaims that "here . . . was born the Republican Party."

Courtesy: Mrs. Howard Rouse

MASS MEETING!

AT MASON, SEPT. 9th, 1854.

To the People of Ingham County, without distinction of Party:

In view of the recent action of Congress in regard to the organization of Nebraska and Kansas Territories, and the evident designs of the Slave power to attempt still further aggressions upon Freedom, we invite all our Fellow Citizens, without reference to former political associations, who think that the time has arrived for a Union at the North, to protect Liberty from being overthrown and down-trodden, to assemble in

Mass Convention,

On Saturday, the 9th day of September next, at 10 o'clock A. M., at the Court House, in the Village of Mason, for the purpose of putting in nomination suitable persons to fill the County offices, Representative to the State Legislature, delegates to the Congressional and Senatorial Conventions, and to transact such other business as may be deemed expedient.

D. G. McClure, J. W. Holmes, W. Jones, Geo. W. Dart, R. Foster, W. Foster, C. O. Stiles, G. A. Brown, J. W. Soule, A. W. Williams, H A. Rueght, D. M. Bagley, M. K. North, H. Bisby, J. O. Smith, C. Thomas, H. H. North, Roswell Everitt, O. D. Skinner, Joshua North, H. Lester, F. R. West, J. Paul, M. T Hicks, R Stephens, W M Stephens, H. D. Granger, J. D. Reeves, A. P. Hicks, A. H. Roble, S. S. Green, C. E. Royce, David Hale, R. Howell, k. Johnson, J. N. Bush, H. Baker, H. L. Baker, J P. Powell, O. D. Parker, E. C. Barker, S. Lovell, J. H. Lobdell, J. W. Demerest, W. S. Calkins, James I. Mead, J. Robson, L. D. Quackinbush, E N. Grilley, S. A. Tooker, A. Nois, S. Harrington, A. Cline, S Sanderson, S Dunn, J W Phelps, John Dansbach, Jr, Sanford Marsh, Geo Smith, Levi Buck, Geo Chappell, Z L Holmes, Thos Treat, C White, B Bristol, W H Child, U Converse S R Wilcox, S Cromsan, S B Wessels, N Parks, J W Bell, Wm Tanner, D J Cobb, E F Thompson, N Bruce, A Otis, Wm Baldwin, L Merrill, L H Spencer, W F Lindsey, E V Van Epps, E W Coolidge, W B Holdreth, T Lester, E W Burdick J T Iroh, S Hoth, J E North, J North, S Barton, S R Greene, Wm Lee, W H Puckney, H B Stoach, O B Webster, S D Newbro, E P Newbro, A B Bagley, N C Branch, U M Chappell, C C Darling, John G Darling, W. K. Everitt.

August 30th, 1854.

Similar meetings, on a smaller scale, were held throughout Michigan in 1854, drawing antislavery Democrats, Whigs, and Free-Soilers together into a new party.

The Michigan Republicans nominated as their gubernatorial candidate Kinsley Bingham of Livingston County, a former Democratic congressman whose antislavery views now brought him into the new party, which he led to victory in 1854, defeating his old Democratic colleague John S. Barry.

Two years later, in 1856, Bingham ran for re-election on a ticket headed by John C. Fremont, the first Republican presidential candidate.

[Right column — campaign ticket:]

Ward 6

THE CONSTITUTION AND THE UNION.
FREMONT AND DAYTON.

Republican

For Electors of President and Vice President of the United States.
FERNANDO C. BEAMAN,
HARMON CHAMBERLIN,
CHAUNCEY H. MILLEN,
WILLIAM H. WITHEY,
OLIVER JOHNSON,
THOMAS J. DRAKE.
  For Governor,
KINSLEY S. BINGHAM.
  For Lieutenant Governor,
GEORGE A. COE.
  For Secretary of State,
JOHN McKINNEY.
  For Auditor General,
WHITNEY JONES.
  For State Treasurer,
SILAS M. HOLMES.
  For Attorney General,
JACOB M. HOWARD.
For Superintendent of Public Instruction,
IRA MAYHEW.
For Commissioner of the State Land Office
SEYMOUR B. TREADWELL.
For Member of State Board of Education,
GEORGE WILLARD.
For Representative in Congress, 1st District,
WILLIAM A. HOWARD.
For Senator in State Legislature, 2d District,
GEORGE JEROME.
For Representatives in the State Legislature
  —1st District,
JAMES M. EDMUNDS,
JOHN BLOYNK,
SYLVESTER LARNED,
CHARLES DOMINE,
MARK FLANIGAN.
  For Sheriff,
JOSEPH EVANS.
  For County Clerk,
WELLINGTON WILLITS.
  For Register of Deeds,
MAHLON S. FROST.
  For County Treasurer,
WILLIAM HARSHA.
  For Judge of Probate,
GEORGE W. SWIFT.
  For Prosecuting Attorney,
HENRY D. TERRY.
  For County Auditor,
ABRAM FISHER.
  For Circuit Court Commissioners,
LYMAN COCHRANE,
HENRY M. CHEEVER.
  For County Surveyor,
EPHRAIM A. SHAW,

On August 26, 1856, a Republican campaign rally was held in Kalamazoo's Bronson Park, shown here in a nineteenth-century photograph. One of the orators on this occasion who spoke from the old Indian mound on which the girl in the photograph stands, was Abraham Lincoln of Illinois. He disappointed his more radical listeners by his position on the slavery question, which they felt was too mild. This may have been one of the reasons why Lincoln never spoke in Michigan again.

Courtesy: Kalamazoo Public Museum

Courtesy: National Archives

There was nothing mild about the antislavery views of Zachariah Chandler, a Detroit merchant who had been the unsuccessful Whig candidate for governor in 1852 and then two years later had been one of the leaders of the group that organized the Republican Party. In 1857, Chandler succeeded Lewis Cass in the United States Senate. Like Cass, Chandler had been born in New Hampshire, and like Cass, who had dominated his party in Michigan for decades, Chandler would dominate Michigan Republican politics until his death in 1879. As this Mathew Brady photograph suggests, Chandler was a grim, fire-eating partisan, who would lead the Radicals in Congress in violent opposition to many of Lincoln's policies during the Civil War and to those of Andrew Johnson in the post-war years.

As the fifties drew to a close, events moved toward the final break between the North and the South. In March, 1859, John Brown, an activist *par excellence* among abolitionists, arrived in Detroit with a dozen slaves he had helped escape from Missouri. In this house on Congress Street, long since torn down, Brown met with the Negro leader, Frederick Douglass, and several members of Detroit's Negro community, including the owner of the house, William Webb.

The group certainly discussed the question of slavery, although there is little solid evidence to substantiate the tradition that Brown at this time outlined his plans to attack Harper's Ferry later that year.

133

POLITICAL DEMONSTRATIONS OF THE PRESIDENTIAL CAMPAIGN TREMENDOUS GATHERING OF REPUBLICANS IN DETROIT ON SEPTEMBER 4, 1860. PROCESSION OF THE WIDE AWAKES From a Sketch by Mr. Lum, of Detroit. (See page 310.)

Courtesy: Burton Historical Collection

In the fateful year of 1860, the rising tide of support in the North for the Republican Party, as evidenced by this parade of "Wide-Awakes" in Detroit on September 4, resulted in the election of the Republican presidential candidate, Abraham Lincoln.

In Michigan, Austin Blair, a Jackson attorney, a strong antislavery man, and a veteran of many political campaigns since coming to Michigan from New York in 1841, was elected governor on the Republican ticket. The office was then only a part-time job, with an annual salary of $1,000. The duties were so light, however, that the governor had ample opportunity to carry on his private business at home, without even bothering to reside in the state capital except during the brief legislative session, normally held every two years. But for Blair the governorship would be no sinecure. Barely three months after he took office, he would suddenly be faced with responsibilities and duties beyond anything his predecessors had encountered. Blair handled them well and was ever after affectionately known as Michigan's "War Governor." But while he was earning this title he had to forget about his law practice and, honest man that he was, he left office virtually impoverished.

The Civil War

Courtesy: Michigan Historical Collections

FROM WASHINGTON.

Correspondence of the N. Y. Times.

Washington, April 11.

I learn that during Ben McCullough's recent visit to this neighborhood, he was in the habit of stopping nights at the house of a prominent banker of this city, retiring to Virginia early in the morning; also that, while here, he was in consultation with the Commissioners, and with leading Secessionists of the district, and of Virginia and Maryland. The authorities have their eye on the man, who, by sheltering this traitor and his co-conspirators, has implicated him in their treason; and his money will not save him if he is not careful.

The lines are being closely drawn in Washington. Under the direction of Cameron and Gen. Scott, well-known sympathisers, and suspected men connected with the secession movement will now be closely watched. It is claimed that the calling out of the District Militia was not all influenced by the reports of McCullough's movements. There are more dangerous and desperate men than he already detected in plots against the peace of the city. He is appreciated by the Government as a very clever and noisy humbug, and thus far his movements in Virginia have amounted to nothing, and probably will not. Many regard this call upon volunteers in this vicinity as an experiment to ascertain the state of public feeling here. The Government is gratified to find so healthy a tone here.

Mr Lincoln, and the great majority of the Cabinet who entertain the policy inaugurated, are receiving hourly assurances of the favor with which that policy is received. The North seems a unit, but it is not the North alone that sends the most hearty commendations. Strange as it may seem, the Border States are quite as earnest as the North. They seem to hail the positive position of the Administration as a prospective bulwark, protecting them from the desolation, anarchy, and taxation of secession. I shall be much mistaken, if the results do not prove that a firm maintenance of the rights of the General Government is the sole of preventive Border State secession.

Notwithstanding the denials of the *Herald*, I renew my assertion, given a week ago, that the great Powers cordially respond to the efforts making by Mr. Lincoln to maintain the integrity of the Union. The assurances of sympathy and concurrence have been more positive and clear than the usual language of diplomacy.—Though unofficially given, they are none the less reliable and satisfactory.

The idea prevalent that the Government has no power to accept volunteers, or to call for aid from the States, or that it lacks authority to use all the reserved forces of the country, is an entire mistake. The Government has no doubt of its legal right to enforce the laws and to collect revenue, in such manner as the exigencies of the case may demand—by blockade or otherwise. No Cabinet that has existed for years embraces more legal talent that of Mr. Lincoln, and on that point it is a unit.

Washington, April 12.

The Commissioners from Virginia arrived in this city this morning, and during the afternoon they visited the President, but not in the official capacity, and were received by him directly after the Cabinet meeting had adjourned.

It is denied that any portion of the Confederate States loan has been offered in New York. More than the entire amount has been arranged at par, within the limits of the Southern Confederacy.

Richmond, April 12.

Hon. Jno. Tyler received this A. M. from Montgomery copies of official despatches between Gen. Beauregard, Major Anderson, and the Secretary of War, Walker.—These were printed and circulated.

Washington, April 12.

The President has directed that Capt. Wm. B. St. Johns, 3d infantry, and Lieut. Abner Smead, 1st artillery, cease to be officers of the army.

The regular troops here have been ordered and proceeded to the outskirts of the city watch every avenue thereto, while the volunteers recently mustered to guard the armories and public building. Videttes are constantly seen riding through the streets. There is comparatively but little excitement here relative to affairs at Charleston.

Washington, April 14.

Efforts are still making to concentrate a formidable military force in and around Washington, to be prepared for all emergencies. Information continues to be received from private sources, of several plots in various localities in Maryland and Virginia, having in view the seizure of the public property and even the persons of the highest officers of the Government. Though these accounts are not generally credited, they are believed in official quarters, and hence the precautionary movements. At all events they are considered necessary, no one knowing what turn events may take during the prevalent excitement.

Roads and avenues leading to Washington are closely watched.

Washington, April 14.

Senator Douglas called on the President to-night. He had an interesting conversation on the present condition of the country. The substance of it was, on the part of Mr. Douglas, that while he was unalterably opposed to the Administration on all its political issues, he was prepared to sustain the President in the exercise of all his constitutional functions to preserve the Union, maintain the Government, and defend the Federal Capital. Firm policy and prompt action were necessary. The Capital of our country is in danger and must be protected at all hazards, at any expense of men and money. He spoke of the present and future, without reference to the past.

Mr. Lincoln was very much gratified with the interview.

Official advices from Montgomery intimate that the Confederate Congress on reassembling will at once declare war against the United States. It is believed that in the act of declaration, a distinction will be made between the alien friends and alien enemies; the former including the Border States, and such citizens of the North as oppose a coercive administration.

THE ATTACK ON SUMTER!

THE SURRENDER!

THE BOMBARDMENT AND DEFENSE!

Effect of the News in Washington

ABSURD AND CONTRADICTORY RUMORS!

PRESIDENT LINCOLN'S PROCLAMATION!

CALLS FOR THE STATE MILITIA!

Action of the States!

The Prevailing Excitement—Thrilling War News—Preparations for War!

The Union Sentiment in Baltimore is Strong—New York and Pennsylvania Act Promptly in Furnishing Assistance to the Government—Senator Douglas is Prepared to Sustain the President—He Recommends a Firm Policy and Prompt Action—War Soon to be Formally Declared by the South—There is an Absurd Rumor of the Resignation of Gen. Scott—Another Blast from George N. Sanders—Jeff. Davis' Answer to the President's Proclamation—Active Recruiting in Buffalo, Toledo, Milwaukee, and other Places—Massachusetts to Draft Her Quota of Troops To-Day—Increased Secession Clamor in Virginia—Lieut. Slemmer is Ordered not to Wait for an Attack if Attempts are Made to Strengthen the Position of his Besiegers—Tenders of Troops have been made to the Government from all Quarters—The President's Proclamation was Unfavorably Received in the South—Union Sentiment in Philadelphia is Strong—Kentucky Refuses to Respond to the Call for Troops—Secession Dead in New Mexico—Concentration of Troops at the Capital.

Charleston, April 14.

The firing ceased at half past one o'clock, and an unconditional surrender made. *The Carolinians are surprised that the fight was over so soon.*

After the flag-staff was shot away, Wigfall was sent by Gen. Beauregard to Sumter with a white flag, offering assistance to subdue the flames. He was met by Anderson, who said he "had just displayed the white flag, but the batteries had not stopped firing." Wigfall replied that Anderson must haul down the American flag.—"Surrender or fight was the word." Anderson hauled down his flag.

Gen. Beauregard's staff came over and stipulated that the surrender should be unconditional for the present, subject to conditions with Beauregard. Anderson is allowed to remain in actual possession for the present.

Charleston, April 14.

Negotiations were completed last night. Anderson's command will evacuate the Fort this morning, and embark on the war vessels now off the harbor. Five of Anderson's men were wounded, one, it is thought, mortally.

After the surrender a boat with ten men was sent from a sloop-of-war outside to Morris Island, requesting permission for the vessel to enter and take off Anderson's command.

It is reported that Anderson surrendered because the officers' quarters and barracks were destroyed, and he had no hope of reinforcement. The fleet lay by 30 hours, and could not, or would not, help him. His men were prostrated by over exertion.

The explosions which were heard in Sumter were caused by a lot of shells ignating. The barracks caught fire three times from hot shot thrown from Fort Moultrie. Everything is in ruins but the casements. Many guns were dismantled, and the walls look like honey-comb. Fort Moultrie is badly damaged, and the houses on the Island are riddled.

A boat was sent from the fort to-night to officially notify the fleet of the surrender of Fort Sumter. It is not known what will be done with Sumter or the vanquished.

Charleston, Sunday, April 14.

Major Anderson and his men will leave to-night on the Isabel for New York. The fleet is still outside.

Charleston, April 13.

The cannonading to-day is going on fiercely from all points, from the vessels out-side, and along the coast. It is reported that Fort Sumter is on fire.

Charleston, April 13—10:30 A. M.

At intervals of twenty minutes firing was kept up all night on Fort Sumter. Major Anderson ceased firing from Fort Sumter at six in the evening. All night he was engaged in repairing damages and protecting the barbette guns. He commenced to return the fire at seven o'clock this morning.

Fort Sumter seems to be greatly disabled. The battery on Cummings' Point does Fort Sumter great damage.

At 9 o'clock this morning a dense smoke poured out from Fort Sumter.

The Federal flag is at half mast, signaling distress.

The shells from Fort Moultrie and the batteries on Morris' Island fall into Major Anderson's stronghold thick and fast, and they can be seen in their course from the Charleston battery.

New York, April 13.

Dispatches received from Col. Waite, commander of the Texan forces, state that a strong Union feeling is growing. Gov. Houston predicts the return of the secessionists to their allegiance. They are terribly taxed. Houston has been offered armed support by Germans in every part of the State, but declined it.

A Washington dispatch to the *Tribune* says: "Capt. Fox commands the vessel with provisions which is to lead the expedition into Charleston.

"The President received the war news calmly, and with a confidedut feeling that he had done his duty in the matter.

"Senator Sherman arrived from Ohio, and reports the Republicans are ready to stand by to the last.

"The opinion prevails that an attempt will be made before sunrise to run the light draft vessels of the fleet up to Sumter reinforce and provision it."

Norfolk, April 13.

The war news from Charleston creates a profound sensation in this city and throughout the State. The general sentiment is that the Federal Government is right and shall be sustained.

Washington, April 13.

The war news are received here with feelings of regret. There is no excitement, but the prospect for the future creates a general feeling of depression.

Providence, R. I., April 13.

Gov. Sprague has tendered to the Government the services of the marine artillery and 1,000 infantry and officers and to accompany them himself.

Savannah, Ga., April 13th.

The lights at Tybee and in this harbor have been discontinued for the present.

Montgomery, April 13.

The President and Secretary of War were screnaded last night. The latter was called out. He said that the Confederate flag would soon be waving over Fort Sumter, and the Federal Capitol at Washington, if the independence of the Southern States was not recognized and if hostilities continued. The only dispatch received last night was from Gen. Beauregard, and is believed to be favorable.

Washington, Sunday, April 14.

The President will issue a proclamation to-morrow, calling for seventy-five thousand militia to suppress the combination in the seceded States.—The United States laws will be duly executed. The first service will probably be to re-possess the forts which have been seized from the Union. The proclamation also convenes Congress to meet on the fourth of July.

The War Department is busy preparing details to communicate to the States.

Washington, Sunday, April 14.

The President's proclamation says: "Whereas, laws of the United States have been, and are now, opposed in several States by combinations too powerful to be suppressed in the ordinary way, I therefore call forth the Militia of the Several States of the Union to the aggregate number of SEVENTY-FIVE THOUSAND, to suppress the said combination, and to execute the laws. I appeal to all loyal citizens to facilitate and aid this effort to maintain the laws, and the integrity of the National Union, and the perpetuity of popular government, and to redress wrongs long enough endured. The first services assigned to the forces will probably be to re-possess the forts, places and property which have been seized from the Union. The utmost care will be taken consistent with these objects to avoid devastation and destructive interference with the property of peaceful citizens in any part of the country; and I hereby command those persons composing the aforesaid combinations to disperse within twenty days from this date.

"I hereby convene both Houses of Congress for the fourth of July next to determine such measures as the public safety and interest demand.

"ABRAHAM LINCOLN, President.

"By W. H. SEWARD, Secretary of State."

Washington, Sunday, April 14.

Arrangements are made to concentrate the military at once at all threatened points. The greatest anxiety exists to hear further Southern news.—It is rumored that an attack will be attempted upon Fort Delaware, Md.—The War Department has taken steps to prevent it.

Five officers of the Navy tendered their resignations to-day, but they were refused, and their names will probably be stricken from the Navy list. The National Volunteers passed resolutions denouncing the military operations of the government, and expressing sympathy with the secessionists. The guards at the departments have been largely increased.

Columbus, Ohio, Sunday, April 14.

Adjutant-General Carrington, has just issued orders, carrying into effect the military laws just enacted by the General Assembly of Ohio, and providing for 6,000 regular militia, besides the militia of reserve of not less than 35,000 men, to be subject to immediate transfer into the regular force. The regular militia has been organized into 25 regiments, which upon a war basis would make 25,000 men.—On Saturday his office was thronged by persons eagerly inquiring for the news, and offering their services irrespective of party to support the general government.

Philadelphia, Sunday, April 14.

Gov. Curtin has gone to Washington. He says Pennsylvania can send 100,000 men to defend Washington.

Indianapolis, Sunday, April 14.

Gov. Morton is in possession of information from all parts of the State, indicating that volunteer companies are being formed everywhere, and that THIRTY THOUSAND men can be relied on to respond to any call for services to defend the national flag.

Chicago, Sunday, April 14.

Gov. Yates will issue a proclamation to-morrow, calling an extra session of the Legislature of Illinois to meet at Springfield a week from next Tuesday.

Alexandria, Va., April 14.

A meeting was held to form a home guard. Resolutions to resist Northern aggression were adopted. Several speakers advocated secession; others argued in favor of coercion to unite the Border States.

New York, April 14.

Advices from Albany state that Gov. Morgan will to-morrow issue a call for 25,000 men for the assistance of our Federal Government.

A private letter from Gov. Curtin and a prominent citizen of New York states that he can have 100,000 Pennsylvanians in Washington in 48 hours, if required.

Philadelphia, April 14.

The reported project to seize Fort Delaware causes much excitement. It is now commanded by Captain Porter, of Virginia, who, it is reported, designs to resign if Virginia secedes.

Fort Mifflin, in Pennsylvania, is a dilapidated affair, now in charge of Sergeant Bromley and one man. The naval magazine adjoining Fort Mifflin is in charge of Mr. Bunker, a veteran of 60 years' service.

Volunteers are making preparations so as to be ready to respond instantly to the call of the Governor or President. Two new regiments are forming, to consist of 1,000 men each, to arm which a portion of the State appropriation will be required.

Our volunteers never have been properly supplied with arms, and frequently new companies had to borrow guns, to parade with, from others better supplied.

Mayor Henry offers his services as Colonel of a regiment if a call is made by the Government.

Washington, April 13.

The President has appointed Earl Bill as Marshal of the Northern District of Ohio.

Baltimore, April 15.

The Union feeling here is strong.—This morning, the Minute Men organization of 2,500 strong, who have been drilling ever since the Presidential election as a military organization, threw out the stars and stripes from their headquarters, with the motto, "The Union and the Constitution."

New York, April 15.

The *Times*' Washington correspondent says the War Department is engaged in calculating the quota of troops in each State. New York will be entitled to ten regiments.

No detailed policy relative to closing Southern ports is yet selected, but arrangements are making to cut off all communication by sea.

Gen. Scott is actively at work calculating the disposition of the troops.

The Administration has reliable information that the Confederate States propose, after reducing Sumter, march on Washington with 20,000 men.

Several additional companies of regulars are ordered to Washington.

The *World's* Washington despatch says: "Detachments of cavalry are stationed on all roads outside the city, and two volunteer companies are in the capitol, one at the Post-office department, and one at the patent office."

Two officers of New York regiments have tendered their commands.

The present indications are that Sumter will be retaken at all hazards.

The New York *Herald's* special despatch from Charleston says: "Anderson saluted his flag, formed his command on the parade ground, and marched out on the wharf, the drum and fife playing Yankee Doodle. During the salute a pile of cartridges burst in one of the casemates, killing two and wounding four men. One of them was buried in the Fort with military honors; the other will be buried by the Carolinians. The wounded men will be taken to Charleston.

The fort was burned to a mere shell. The guns on one side of the parapet are entirely dismantled, and others split, and the gun carriages knocked to splinters. Anderson is reported to have ordered not to sight the men but to silence the batteries.

Sumter has been garrisoned by the Palmetto guards, under command of Col. Ripley.

The fire has again broke out in the ruins of the fort and the engines have been sent down.

Boston, April 15.

Political differences have been dropped and the universal sentiment of the city and State is, to defend to the last the flag of the Union.

Volunteers to the number of 20,000 have already tendered their services at the Adjutant General's office.

Gen. B. F. Butler, an ardent supporter of Breckenridge during the election, has tendered his services with his entire brigade.

Washington April 15.

The War Department has accepted the Governor of Rhode Island's offer of a regiment, and that they be sent on to Washington without delay.

Three regiments in the District of Columbia tendered their services to the government to-day.

Maine, New Hampshire, Vermont, Rhode Island, Conneticut, Delaware, Arkansas, Michigan, Wisconsin, Iowa, Minnesota, are to furnish one regiment each. New York 17 regiments, Pennsylvania 16 regiments, Ohio 13 regiments; New Jersey, Maryland, Kentucky, Missouri, four regiments each; Illinois and Indiana six regiments each; Virginia three regiments.

It is ordered that each regiment shall consist on an aggregate of officers and men of 780—73,320 men. The remainder, which constitutes 75,000 under the Presidents proclamation, will be composed of troops in the District of Columbia.

Hon. John Covode has offered Gov. Curtin $50,000 of the loan authorised by Pennsylvania, to arm and equip the troops ordered by the State.

A delegation of Pittsburgh merchants have made a similar tender.

Special dispatch to the Chicago Tribune

Washington, April 15.—The Government acts with great energy and dispatch. Preparations are making on the grandest scale for the suppression of the Southern rebellion. The Government will not limit itself to the number of volunteers called for, but will accept all the several States may offer. Up to this morning nearly one hundred thousand men were offered by telegraph by Northern Governors and commanding officers.

Scott thinks twenty-five thousand men will concentrate here by the first of May.

Gov. Sprague's offer of one thousand men was accepted. The troops are expected on Thursday.

All forts, arsenals and armories in Virginia, Maryland, Kentucky and Missouri will immediately receive strong garrisons.

The Philadelphia Banks telegraphed to Gov. Curtin here, tendering all the money he wanted for arming the State.

A number of eye witnesses to the bombardment of Fort Sumter have arrived here. All agree that Major Anderson fought bravely and earnestly, and did much more damage than was reported. Several insist on having seen boat-loads of dead and wounded brought in from the rebel batteries.

No more resignations in the army and navy will be accepted after this. Recusants will be court-martialed.

Cassius M. Clay has arrived. He thinks Unionism in Kentucky is in the ascendant, but fears a conflict between Unionists and Secessionists in that State.

Washington bears a decidedly warlike aspect. The streets are full of soldiers.—Recruiting parties, with long files behind them, marched up and down the avenues to the tune of fife and drum all day.

MAY APPOINTMENT.

DR. V. C. Price, Analytical Physician of Buffalo, N. Y., will be for consultation on diseases generally at

MARSHALL, Herndon House, Wednesday, the 8th of May.

KALAMAZOO, Burdick House, May 9th.

[illegible]

MARSHALL STATESMAN.

Wednesday, April 17, 1861.

THE CRISIS IN DETROIT.

A Preliminary Meeting for the Purpose of Obtai[ning] an Expression of the Sentiment of our Ci[ti]zens upon the Questions now before the Ame[r]ican People.

The Chair stated that he had desire[d] Mr. Frazer to preside, in order that he (th[e] Chair) might offer a few resolutions. B[ut] as he had them prepared he would offe[r] them, notwithstanding his position. The[y] were as follows:

Resolved, That we do most solemnly, [in] view of the difficulty in which our muc[h] beloved country is plunged, pledge ou[r] lives, our property, and our sacred hono[r] to sustain the Government of the Unite[d] States, in preserving the Union, executin[g] the laws, and suppressing rebellion an[d] treason wherever manifested.

Resolved, That to the utmost of our abi[lity] "The Star Spangled Banner shall tr[i]umphantly wave o'er the land of the fre[e] and the home of the brave."

Resolved, That Michigan now takes h[er] stand in favor of the Constitution and th[e] laws of the nation, and REPUDIATES th[e] TREASON that secession can for one momen[t] be countenanced.

Resolved, That come what may in th[e] events of the future, WE stand by the Go[v]ernment, and will give our most cordi[al] support and most earnest devotion to up[hold] the Union and the Constitution [of] 1787, and do respectfully request our Sta[te] Executive to adopt immediate measures [to] exhibit the adhesion of Michigan to ou[r] Constitution and our Union.

Mr. Romeyn offered the following:

Resolved, that a Committee of ten be a[p]pointed by the Chair to call a meeting [of] the citizens of Detroit, without distinctio[n] of party, at such time and place as the[y] may deem advisible, with a view to expre[ss] the sentiment of this community in refe[r]ence to the conflict in which the Gover[n]ment of the United States is now forced [to] engage with the treasonable and rebelliou[s] organization which has assumed the nam[e] of the Confederate States.

We copy the above resolutions offere[d] by the Hon. Ross Wilkins, of Detroit, a[s] being indicative of the state of feeling every[where] where existing among the loyal part of th[e] people of the United States.

In a time like this, when delibera[te] treason stalks abroad over the land, and parricidal hand has made war upon one o[f the] best governments that ever existed—ther[e] is no neutral ground. Every true man who has been protected by our laws, an[d] enjoyed the peaceful security of our Con[stitution], is bound to come to the rescue o[f] his country, or suffer the brand of infamy which now attaches to the name of Bene[dict] Arnold.

We have a Government, glorious in i[ts] mission beyond any other in existence simply, because it proclaims security an[d] liberty, freedom and equality to every citi[zen] thereof. And it is because of this ver[y] principle, this glorious reality, that a set o[f] miscreants, who will be infamous to a[ll] eternity, have struck at its vitality, an[d] seek to establish on its ruins, a governmen[t] whose foundation is to be laid deep an[d] strong, upon the idea or principle, "tha[t] slavery, subordination to the superior rac[e] is the natural and normal condition of part of mankind."

Will they succeed in turning back th[e] spirit of a Christian civilization? We sha[ll] see.

We copy the above resolutions, and refe[r] to the spirited speeches, by Messrs. Wil[kins], Frazer, Lothrop, Buel, and othe[r] prominent Democrats, of Detroit, as well a[s] the Republicans present, to show the littl[e] club of disunion traitors in this city, num[bering] eight or ten, who rejoice at the downfall of Fort Sumter, and the disgrac[e] it attaches to the American Flag and name that *they are solitary and alone in their ef[forts] to obtain unenviable infamy* and t[o] warn them that they will be alone in thei[r] efforts to create a "fire in the rear."

Their partizan zeal and their hatred o[f] Republicanism, has beguiled them of thei[r] reason, and we simply advise them, tha[t] with Hon. R. Wilkins as Judge, and wa[r] existing by the mad acts of South Carolin[a] and slavery, a very little aid and comfor[t] to the enemy would constitute treason an[d] receive a traitor's doom.

Slavery has already accomplished a pa[rt] of its mission, it has produced a state o[f] barbarism at the South, which is the nec[essary] and inevitable work—this barbarism alone implies its votaries to sack, to destroy and make waste and desolation reign on the land.

It has provoked and made an unholy war because the spirit of freedom would no[t] yield to their debasing demands—but than[k] God, patriotism has not all vanished.—Pennsylvania says 100,000 men for liberty Ohio, New York,—the New England States say 300,000 men for liberty; the grea[t] north-west, who owe their unprecedente[d] success to the spirit of liberty, invkoed fo[r] her benefit, by its great apostle Jefferson,—says 100,000 men, for liberty, and we pledg[e] our honor, that if this means fail, that ou[r] heroic mothers, sisters, and daughters woul[d] meet the enemy upon such a cause and beat them back.

We much mistake the temper of our ga[l]lant executive, if he does not tender th[e] national resources of the State to sustai[n] our Government.

We congratulate the citizens o[f] Battle Creek and vicinity upon the ap[pointment] of JUDGE HALL to be Post Mas[ter] of that city. Judge Hall has long bee[n] regarded as one of the purest and ables[t] men in the county, a thorough business man prompt and active, yet, at the same time, a model of urbanity and politeness. Of cours[e] with such qualifications, the duties of th[e] office will be both faithfully and acceptabl[y] performed.

APPOINTED.—Col. Dickey has appointed as deputies Mr. Charles T. Dickey, of Mar[shall]; Mr. Thomas Alexander, Jr., o[f] Dexter, and Mr. Joseph R. Bennett, o[f] Adrian. These, with the appointment o[f] Mr. Henry B. Brown, of Detroit, are th[e] only ones that Col. Dickey has made.—*De[troit] Tribune.*

In 1861, screaming headlines of the type familiar to modern newspaper readers were as yet undreamed of, but the firing on Fort Sumter and the subsequent surrender of that federal post in South Carolina was an event of such obvious importance that no reader of the Marshall *Statesman* or any other Michigan paper of that day needed any assistance to realize the momentous nature of these events. War had broken out—a civil war that would disrupt the union of which Michigan had been a voting member for less than twenty-five years.

Throughout Michigan, public meetings were held to voice the concern of the citizens and to express their united support of the federal government's initial steps to combat the rebellion of the Southern states. At this April 20th meeting on Detroit's Griswold Street, public officials of the federal, state, county, and city governments renewed their oaths of allegiance, as a great crowd, some of them standing on roofs and ledges, looked on. In the background is the old capitol building. The Detroit photographer J. Jex Bardwell recorded this and other wartime events in Detroit, providing the first extended photographic record of any phase of Michigan's history.

By the end of April, the first Michigan troops were assembling, in response to President Lincoln's call upon the states to supply the federal government with the forces needed to put down the revolt. In contrast with the wars of the twentieth century when the task of filling the manpower needs of the nation's armed services has been directed primarily from Washington, in the nineteenth century it was the states who were given the major responsibility for raising troops for the army. During the Civil War, Michigan would furnish nearly sixty military units of infantry,

cavalry, artillery, and miscellaneous other types, each of which was designated throughout the war as a Michigan outfit, although serving in the Union army. Lincoln first called for men for terms of only three months. The First Michigan Infantry Regiment, composed of previously organized state militia companies, assembled to meet this call and went through a brief training program on the rolling terrain of Fort Wayne, Detroit.

On May 11, a ceremony was held in Campus Martius (one of the areas on Judge Woodward's city plan from which several streets radiate like spokes from the hub of a wheel) at which the First Michigan received its regimental colors. Hiram Andrews' Rail-road Hotel provided a good vantage point from which to view the proceedings. Two days later, the regiment shipped out for Washington and war service.

137

Scarcely a week after it arrived in Washington, the First Michigan Infantry, which was the first regiment from the Western states to come to the defense of the nation's capital, was leading an advance across the Potomac to capture Alexandria, Virginia. When Michigan subscribers to *Harper's Weekly* opened their June 15 issue, they found this sketch depicting Confederate cavalrymen surrendering to the regiment.

COMPANY OF SECESSION CAVALRY SURRENDERING TO COLONEL WILCOX, OF THE FIRST MICHIGAN REGIMENT, IN FRONT OF THE SLAVE-PEN AT ALEXANDRIA, VIRGINIA.—[DRAWN BY OUR SPECIAL ARTIST.]

Courtesy: Burton Historical Collection

Courtesy: Burton Historical Collection

The members of the First Michigan Infantry were not gone from Michigan very long. Their three-month term of enlistment having expired, they arrived back in Detroit on August 2 on board a flag-decorated train of the Detroit and Milwaukee Railroad, the successor to the old Detroit and Pontiac. The crowd that turned out to greet the soldiers was so excited that many of the spectators are only blurs on the photograph which Jex Bardwell took with the slow-speed equipment of the day. (The black line down the middle of the picture is the result of a break in the glass negative.) At the station, Lewis Cass, now nearly eighty years old, made a welcoming address to Michigan's first Civil War veterans. They had acquitted themselves well in the Union army's disastrous defeat at Bull Run, and although many of the officers joined other Michigan regiments, most of the enlisted men decided to quit while they were ahead and returned to civilian life.

138

Below:

Meanwhile, other military units were being formed. The Second Michigan Infantry was mustered into federal service at Fort Wayne on May 25, 1861, as Michigan's first regiment to enlist for the three-year term which now became standard. Its commander was Colonel Israel B. Richardson of Pontiac, a West Point graduate, a man itching to lead his troops into battle, as this superb Brady portrait reveals. He got his wish. At Antietam in 1862, Richardson, now a division commander, rallied his men with the cry, "Boys! Raise the colors and follow me!" As he advanced, hatless, his sword drawn, Richardson was mortally wounded, but his example inspired his soldiers to drive back the Confederates.

Courtesy: Library of Congress

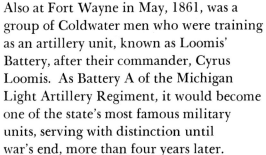

Also at Fort Wayne in May, 1861, was a group of Coldwater men who were training as an artillery unit, known as Loomis' Battery, after their commander, Cyrus Loomis. As Battery A of the Michigan Light Artillery Regiment, it would become one of the state's most famous military units, serving with distinction until war's end, more than four years later.

One of the ten-pounder Parrott guns which the Loomis Battery received when it went south in 1861 is displayed in a park in Coldwater at the junction of US-27 and US-12. The gun was captured by the Confederates in 1863 at the battle of Chickamauga, where the battery suffered its heaviest losses of the war. Later, other Union forces recaptured the gun and returned it to its surviving gunners.

THIRD REGIMENT MICHIGAN VOLUNTEERS MARCHING DOWN JEFFERSON AVENUE, DETROIT, MICHIGAN. Sketched by J. R. Nannert See page 179

Companies and regiments were formed at various points in the state. The Third Michigan Infantry, organized at Grand Rapids, was sketched by an artist for the New York *Illustrated News* as it marched down Jefferson Avenue, Detroit, en route to Virginia. The havelocks that make the men look like something out of a foreign legion movie were one of the exotic uniform styles affected at the outset of the war and soon discarded in favor of more practical battle garb.

In the early days of the war military companies were formed in local communities faster than there were places for them in the regiments the state was organizing. Rather than wait until additional Michigan regiments were created, a number of these companies offered their services to and were accepted by regiments of other states. Such a company was the Lafayette Light Guard of Paw Paw, shown here on the day that it left home to serve as Company C of the Seventieth New York Infantry Regiment.

Probably the most unusual regiment organized in Michigan was the Lancer Regiment, a mounted unit organized by Colonel Arthur Rankin, a veteran of the British army. An artist for *Harper's Weekly* made this sketch late in 1861, showing some of the men with their lances, which were made in Michigan from Michigan white ash. The lances were to be the regiment's principal, if not sole, weapon in battle. However, because Rankin and his men would not comply with army regulations regarding arms and equipment, the regiment was not accepted by the army and had to be disbanded.

COLONEL RANKIN'S LANCER REGIMENT, NOW AT DETROIT, MICHIGAN.—Sketched by B. R. Erman.—[See Page 811.]

Courtesy: Michigan Historical Collections

Although the Lancer Regiment never got into action, eleven regular cavalry regiments were mustered in from Michigan, as, for example, the Fifth Michigan Cavalry. This colorful broadside is typical of those published during the war as souvenirs for soldiers and their families. One wonders, however, how many copies were sold to the twenty-one members of Company H who deserted, particularly to William H. Watson, who appears on the scroll of honor as a two-time deserter. Not every Civil War soldier was a hero.

It was as commander of the Michigan Cavalry Brigade, composed of the First, Fifth, Sixth, and Seventh Michigan Cavalry Regiments, that George Armstrong Custer first won fame as a twenty-three-year-old brigadier general. Custer was born in Ohio, but his family had subsequently moved to Monroe County, Michigan. Custer spent considerable time there and during the war married the daughter of a leading citizen of Monroe. In this Brady photograph, the rakish tilt of the hat, the folded arms, and the facial expression give an inkling of the personality traits which would make Custer one of America's most controversial military figures.

After leaving Michigan, the regiments were sent either to the eastern or western theaters of operation where they spent long months in camp. This was undoubtedly an idealized sketch of the camp of the Sixteenth Michigan Infantry during the winter of 1862-63, after a full year of campaigning in Virginia during the war's second year.

More realistic were the many photographs of Michigan men in camp that were taken by Mathew Brady or his assistants or by some other army photographers. Here a group of men from the Twenty-first Michigan Infantry pose with their Enfield rifles in front of some rather permanent-appearing quarters in their camp in the West where this regiment spent its time during the war.

Courtesy: National Archives

The Fourth Michigan Infantry seems to have been a favorite of the cameramen, judging by the number of photographs of members of this unit that are found in the Brady Collection at the National Archives. With his sword, his Colt revolver tucked in his belt, his mustache, and his erect figure, Lieutenant Henry G. Hill of Company D of the Fourth made a fine picture of a Union officer.

At the other extreme from the trim, assured image of Henry Hill is this splendid photograph of Private Emory Eugene Kingin, who enlisted in the Twenty-first Michigan Infantry early in 1864 at the age of seventeen. The strictly non-regulation checked shirt, the bowie knife, and the nonchalant pose all may have been efforts to cloak the true feelings of a frightened youth.

Courtesy: National Archives

143

The Negro boy, clad in a Union uniform, seated on the ground with these men of the Fourth Michigan, was a familiar sight in the regimental camps in the South as slaves from nearby plantations entered the Union lines. These Michigan men had apparently solved the problem of what to do with this particular boy—a problem which, multiplied by many thousands, was a source of bitter debate among army commanders and government leaders. As the war progressed, however, more and more people in the North began to ask: Weren't young boys like this what the war was all about?

As is the case in every war, there were long hours in which there was nothing to do. Members of Company M of the Fourth Michigan here seem to be demonstrating, somewhat stiffly, to be sure, how they filled these empty hours by smoking, drinking, and card-playing.

The ultimate objective of Michigan's soldiers was to fight and defeat the Confederate armies. These men are identified as members of the Twenty-first Michigan Infantry who had been wounded in battle. Brady identifies the battle as Fair Oaks, which occurred in Virginia on May 31 to June 1, 1862. If this is correct, then Brady's identification of the regiment is in error since the Twenty-first had not been organized by that date, and when it was, it saw action not in Virginia but in the western campaigns.

For these men of the Twenty-fourth Michigan Infantry, the war ended with the battle of Gettysburg. The thirteen or so men who can be counted in this memorable photograph by the great Timothy O' Sullivan were but a small fraction of the total number of casualties that decimated the ranks of the Twenty-fourth and gave it the dubious honor of having suffered heavier losses in this turning point of the war than those of any other Union regiment at Gettysburg.

During the Civil War, more than ninety thousand Michigan men entered the army. The great majority of them volunteered for service, attracted by recruiting posters such as these three from the collection of Norm Flayderman of New Milford, Connecticut. After the initial wave of enthusiasm of the first weeks of the war had passed, however, a variety of inducements, financial and otherwise, had to be resorted to by the organizers of the state's later military units, such as the Seventeenth Michigan Infantry, which needed three months to fill its ranks in 1862.

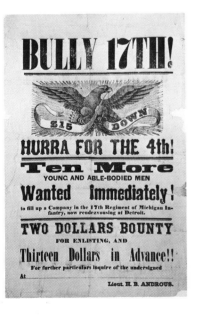

145

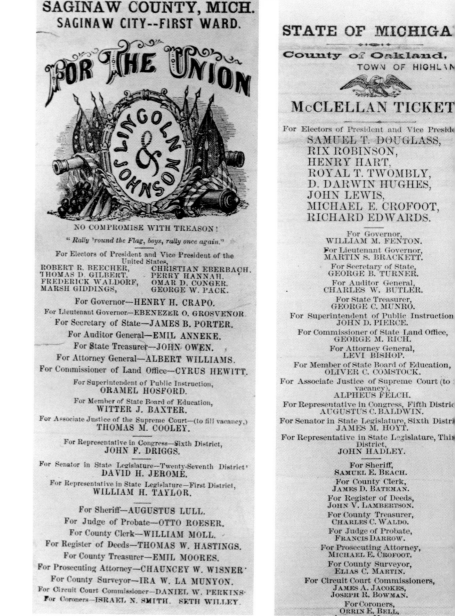

As the war dragged on and the casualty totals swelled (one of every six Michigan soldiers would die as a result of war service), it became ever harder to find volunteers. If all else failed, men might be drafted. But the Civil War draft was a far cry from the military conscription of the twentieth century. The draft was used only if a state failed to fill its assigned quota of troops with volunteers. However, even if a man were drafted, he could be exempted not only for the usual medical or family reasons but also by furnishing a substitute to go in his place, as Cyrus S. Farrar of Armada is hereby certified as having done in 1864, or by paying a commutation fee of $300.

(For description, see caption at the top of next page.)

This was Camp Blair in Jackson, where, beginning in March, 1864, those men who were drafted were inducted into service. The first reception center for draftees had been in Grand Rapids. At the close of the war, Camp Blair would become one of the two principal centers in Michigan where soldiers were paid off and returned to civilian life.

(See the two illustrations at the right-hand top of preceding page.)

In 1864, Michigan's vote helped re-elect Abraham Lincoln to a second term as President, although war weariness gave the Republicans some anxious moments during the campaign. Austin Blair retired after two terms as governor and was succeeded by a Flint lumberman, Henry H. Crapo. On the losing Democratic ticket were such formidable names out of the past as Alpheus Felch, Rix Robinson, and John D. Pierce, Michigan's first superintendent of public instruction under Governor Mason, three decades before. As respected as these men were, they were not able to reverse the trend which would make Michigan a safe Republican state almost continuously for the following seventy years.

In the spring of 1865, the great national testing came to an end. At the beginning of April, after a bitter nine-month siege by Union forces, General Robert E. Lee was forced to abandon the Confederate capital of Richmond, Virginia, with its neighboring stronghold, Petersburg. On April 3, a Michigan brigade, consisting of the Second and Twentieth Michigan Infantry and the First Michigan Sharpshooters Regiments, were the first federal troops to enter Petersburg. Here, an artist for *Harper's Weekly* shows the Second Michigan hoisting its colors over the customs house.

Courtesy: Michigan Historical Collections

Within less than a week after Michigan's soldiers occupied Petersburg, General Lee and his men surrendered at Appomattox Courthouse, and Michigan residents across the state assembled to celebrate the happy news.

SURRENDER OF GEN. LEE!

"The Year of Jubilee has come! Let all the People Rejoice!"

200 GUNS WILL BE FIRED

On the Campus Martius,

AT 3 O'CLOCK TO-DAY, APRIL 10,

To Celebrate the Victories of our Armies.

Every Man, Woman and Child is hereby ordered to be on hand prepared to Sing and Rejoice. The crowd are expected to join in singing Patriotic Songs.

ALL PLACES OF BUSINESS MUST BE CLOSED AT 2 O'CLOCK.

Hurrah for Grant and his noble Army.

By Order of the People.

Within a week, however, the same Detroiters who had met to commemorate Lee's surrender were back in Campus Martius for a solemn observance of the death of President Lincoln from an assassin's bullet.

At Irwinsville, Georgia, on May 10, 1865, the fleeing Confederate president, Jefferson Davis, was captured by the Fourth Michigan Cavalry Regiment. This satirical contemporary sketch accepts the first report by Union officers that Davis was dressed in women's clothes when he was taken. Later, this was denied, and the subject is still a controversial one.

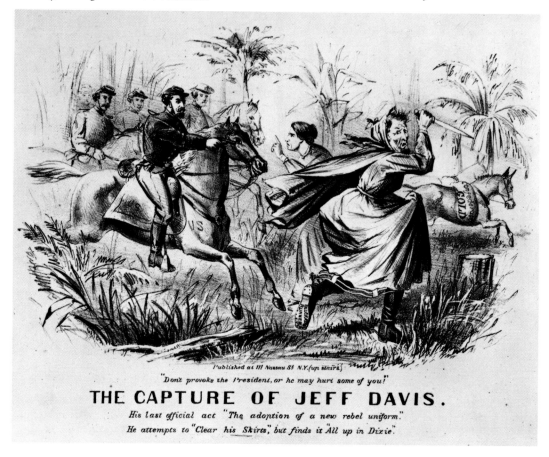

Published at 111 Nassau St. N.Y. (up stairs.)

"Don't provoke the President, or he may hurt some of you!"

THE CAPTURE OF JEFF DAVIS.

His last official act "The adoption of a new rebel uniform".
He attempts to "Clear his Skirts", but finds it "All up in Dixie".

148

Courtesy: Michigan Historical Collections

The year 1865 marked the end of the Civil War. The news of the year was summarized in poetic form in this sheet which the Kalamazoo *Gazette*'s carrier boys distributed to their patrons on January 1, 1866. The "Carrier Boy's Address," issued annually on New Year's day, was a charming custom common to most newspapers in Michigan in the nineteenth century.

Courtesy: Burton Historical Collection

Courtesy: Michigan Historical Collections

On July 4, 1866, with the last Michigan regiments now mustered out of service, Michigan's veterans assembled in Detroit for a great parade that preceded a ceremony in Campus Martius in which each of the state's military units returned to the governor the colors which they had carried into battle. These flags are today preserved in cases in the rotunda of the state capitol in Lansing, and are in many ways the most touching mementos of the sacrifices the young state made in the Civil War.

In the years following the war, determined efforts were made to see that Michigan did not forget the war. The custom of setting aside May 30 each year as a national holiday on which the graves of soldiers would be decorated was begun in 1868. (The observance in 1869 was held on May 29 because the 30th fell on a Sunday.)

Courtesy: Adrian Daily Telegram

Throughout Michigan, monuments began to be erected to the state's Civil War soldiers. The first of these was this simple sandstone shaft, costing $1,500, which was placed in the cemetery at Tipton in Lenawee County and was dedicated on July 4, 1866. (The monument was blown over in the Palm Sunday tornado of 1965 but has since been restored.)

At the foot of Emerald Street in Houghton, this statue since 1912 has served as a reminder of the members of Company I (the Houghton Company) of the Twenty-third Michigan Infantry and of the other men, numbering five hundred in all, from this Upper Peninsula mining county who marched away to war in the 1860's.

Courtesy: Houghton Daily Mining Gazette

This dramatic monument, the work of the distinguished American sculptor Lorado Taft, stands in a small park at First Street and West Michigan and Wildwood Avenues, Jackson. It was donated by one of Jackson's best-known soldiers, William H. Withington, who served with the original First Michigan Infantry at the start of the war, was captured at Bull Run, and returned to Michigan to become colonel of the Seventeenth Michigan Infantry. Unforeseen production problems delayed the actual erection and dedication of the monument until July 14, 1904, despite the date inscribed on the base. By this time, General Withington had died.

Austin Blair, Michigan governor during all but the last few months of the Civil War, died in 1894. The last thirty years of his life had not been especially happy ones for him. He had been denied by the party he had helped to found the office he most desired to hold, the office of United States senator, and for a time in the 1870's he went over to the Democratic Party. His finances continued in such bad condition that in 1892 friends took up a collection of some four thousand dollars which they presented to him at Christmastime as "a little aid, not as charity, but as a token of affection." In 1898 this statue of Blair was erected on state capitol grounds in Lansing, at a cost to the state of $7,200. In the years since its unveiling, the statue, the work of Edward Clark Potter, the same sculptor who also completed the famous equestrian statue of General Custer in Monroe, has acquired the patina and discoloration associated with bronze and has become one of Lansing's most celebrated landmarks.

152

Michigan, the Farm State

During the Civil War, Congress passed the Homestead Act, offering up to 160 acres of public land free to American citizens or aliens who had declared their intention to become citizens, if they lived on the land for five years and began to farm it. The northern two-thirds of Michigan was still largely unsettled at this time, and it was therefore, for a number of years, one of the principal areas in the country to which settlers came to obtain this free land. This photograph, taken at the end of the century, shows what is described as a "typical home" of one of these Michigan homesteaders.

Courtesy: Library of Congress

Agriculture in the nineteenth century was the bulwark of the state's economy. This father and his son, unsmiling in the midst of a hard life but proud of their achievements, were representative of the majority of Michigan residents who made their living from the soil.

Courtesy: Al Barnes

Courtesy: Grand Rapids Public Museum

For those who established this farm near Lowell, and for most Michigan farmers, except those fortunate enough to buy land on one of southern Michigan's scattered and small prairies, clearing the land of its timber cover was a back-breaking task.

154

Courtesy: Michigan Historical Collections

Stump pullers, such as the Little Giant Rock and
Stump Extractor and the home-made but effective model
which these Michigan farmers used, were a welcome aid.

Once they were pulled, the stumps were burned. Sometimes pioneers in southern Michigan, weary of the task of cutting down trees, saved themselves the trouble by simply burning the trees down, destroying hardwood that was potentially of enormous value to the lumberman, but to farmers was only an obstacle which had to be removed if the land was to be plowed and planted.

A scene such as this, photographed near Otsego Lake in 1939, was a strange one in the mechanized twentieth century, but in the nineteenth century the ox-drawn plow was a familiar sight in Michigan, along with the more familiar horse-drawn plow.

155

Courtesy: Michigan State Highway Department

On this pioneer farm near Greenville, in west-central Michigan, a successful grain crop was being harvested laboriously by hand in a field that was still not completely cleared of stumps.

Michigan by the mid-nineteenth century was one of the leading agricultural states in the nation, and wheat and other grains were the main cash crops. This was the scene in Eaton Rapids in the 1870's as the farmers of the area assembled for the wheat market auction.

As the century wore on, however, the diversity that would come to characterize Michigan agriculture was beginning to appear. Farmers in central Michigan, many of them drawing on their New England background, supplemented their regular farm income by tapping the maple trees on their wood lots to obtain sap for maple sugar and maple syrup.

Northern Michigan would become famous for its potatoes.

156

Beginning in the 1890's, sugar beets would become a major crop of the Saginaw Valley and the Thumb, where this photograph was taken in 1939. This region, too, would become the nation's great bean-producing area.

Michigan's most famous specialized agricultural area, however, became a narrow band of land along the Lake Michigan shore of the lower peninsula. Here, due to the moderating effects of the lake's waters and the prevailing westerly winds, warmer year-round temperatures and a longer growing season from that found a few miles farther inland enabled the farmers living here to concentrate on the growing of fruit. Here, in Michigan's Fruit Belt, springtime became one of the most beautiful in America as the great orchards burst into bloom.

These were strawberry pickers near Frankfort, in the northern half of the Fruit Belt.

157

Courtesy: Al Barnes

This elderly, bearded farmer was supervising the packing of apples, grown on a farm at Old Mission, in the Traverse Bay area.

Courtesy: Al Barnes

The Traverse Bay region, however, became most famous for its cherries, such as these people on the Brinkman farm at Old Mission were picking.

In Berrien County in southwestern Michigan, the Fruit Belt reaches its greatest distance inland, some thirty miles, making this county consistently among the most prosperous agricultural counties in the country. At Benton Harbor a great fruit market developed, shown here in the twentieth century, where the products of the area's fruit farms could be sold.

From St. Joseph and Benton Harbor, at the mouth of the St. Joseph River, fruit was shipped across Lake Michigan to Chicago, the same route that later became popular for lake cruises.

Around 1880, histories of most of the counties of southern Michigan were published, which was part of a nation-wide program promoted by several publishing firms who cashed in on the historical interest that was generated in 1876 by the celebration of the centennial of the Declaration of Independence. More than any other group of citizens in the state, Michigan's farmers yielded to the temptation to pay to have their portraits and sketches of their farms appear in these volumes. The farm scenes are invariably as flattering and as idealized as the portraits, on the other hand, are unflattering and starkly realistic in the view they give of their subjects. This was the relatively modest farm of Rodolphus Tryon in Alaiedon Township of Ingham County, together with the portraits of Tryon and his wife, Lavina, which were included in the expensive two-page spread which Tryon paid for in the *History of Ingham and Eaton Counties,* published in Philadelphia in 1880. Tryon, the accompanying biographical sketch declared, had gone heavily in debt when he first moved to Ingham County in 1844, but by this time he had "a well-won competency." The sketch, which was approved, if not written, by Tryon, described the farmer as a man "possessed of many of the virtues and but few of the failings of mankind." His wife was "a lady of more than an ordinary amount of resolution and stamina."

In contrast with the Tryon farm is this view of the farm of George B. Vanatta in the neighboring Ingham County township of Meridian Township. Although their portraits made them look older, the Vanattas were only in their mid-forties and, what was somewhat uncommon at that time, both were natives of Michigan, having been born in Washtenaw County. Vanatta was described as "raising all kinds of farm productions," but, as the sketch makes clear, he was proudest of his livestock, "of which he is an extensive breeder." Some of Vanatta's eight children can be seen in front of the farmhouse, which fortunately was quite large.

159

Levi Arnold of Gun Plain Township in Allegan County was obviously very proud of his Poland China hogs, for in the two-page sketch of his farm which he paid to have printed in the *History of Allegan and Barry Counties,* published in Philadelphia in 1880, he had the artist devote the foreground to portrayals of his prize pigs: Dauntless, Oxford Belle, Lady Broadham (at two years), King of Riversides, Black Nell (weight: 625 pounds), Pride of Michigan, Lady of Oxford, and Victor. An inset provided a close-up of Arnold's piggery and office.

In this view of the S. S. Fairbank's farm near Litchfield, in the *History of Hillsdale County* published at Philadelphia in 1879, the emphasis is on the crops that were grown on the farm.

This was the farm of William Curtis and Sons near Wheatland, also in Hillsdale County. The large house, the many fine farm buildings, the well-landscaped grounds, the cattle in the foreground, and the inset sketch of the tenant's house all denote a prosperous agricultural enterprise.

"Gothic Ridge" was the name which Albert D. Healy gave to his farm at Casco in Allegan County. The house was, in fact, a good example of Gothic-style architecture that was fashionable in the third quarter of the nineteenth century. The farm itself, with Lake Michigan but a short distance away, was given over entirely to fruit growing, with seventeen acres covered with peach trees, 880 plum trees, and six acres of miscellaneous other fruits.

The Hustons established this farm in Galien Township in Berrien County in 1858, two years after they were married. By the time this view appeared in the *History of Berrien and Van Buren Counties,* published at Philadelphia in 1880, farm machinery was assuming an increasingly greater role in farm operations.

This photograph taken on a farm at Mulliken in Eaton County shows a steam threshing machine in operation which is not unlike the one depicted on the Huston farm. At least twenty-two men can be counted who are taking part in the threshing activities.

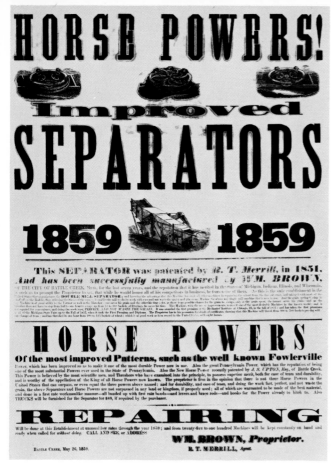

Much of the early manufacturing that developed in Michigan was in response to the need for farm machinery. Here William M. Brown of Battle Creek advertizes the separator he manufactured, which, he boasted, would "thresh from 300 to 700 bushels per day without change of team; and has threshed in one hour from 100 to 125 bushels of wheat; which is as good work as is on record in the United States, with eight horses."

This monstrous contraption, drawn by sixteen horses, was a harvester-combine patented by Hiram Moore of Climax in 1836. In this faded photograph, believed to date from the late 1840's, Moore, in the tall black hat, sits on top of his machine, which was capable of harvesting twenty to thirty acres a day. Lucius Lyon was Moore's financial backer, but defects in the machine, which caused it to break down frequently, and costly lawsuits between Moore and Cyrus H. McCormick over patent rights finally forced Moore to abandon plans to manufacture the harvester.

Despite Hiram Moore's failures, by the end of the nineteenth century machines had taken over much of the work which the early Michigan farmers had done by hand. Here one of them drives a machine that was cutting and binding the corn in his field much faster and more efficiently than it had taken several men to do the same tasks by hand a few years before.

Courtesy: University Archives, Western Michigan University

The changing times were spelled out on Charlie Goodwin's Implement Shop in Colon in the 1880's, a place where farmers of the area could buy McCormick or Champion harvesters, South Bend or Oliver plows, and other equipment. Such shops were now found in every country village.

The mechanization of farm operations marked the passing of the pioneer farming era. With it also gradually disappeared such fine old customs as the barn raising, when relatives and neighbors would gather to build a new barn. . . .

. . . More than 125 men, women, and children can be counted in this group picture. Both pictures date from around the turn of the twentieth century when the practice was still observed in some areas.

Courtesy: Michigan Department of Conservation

Rising farm costs resulting from the use of machines and other factors drove many small farmers out of business and caused scenes such as these to become common, especially in northern Michigan, where poor soil conditions and a short growing season crushed the hopes of thousands of young farm couples who settled in that region in the latter years of the nineteenth century and the early years of the twentieth.

Courtesy: Michigan Historical Collections

164

The Age of the Lumberman

The old man lit up his pipe and recalled the days of his youth when he participated in the final stages of one of the major events in American history: the logging of the immense forests of central and northern Michigan. It had been a rough, rigorous life, but in the tradition of the pioneer period, he and his fellow woodsmen had wrested from the wilderness the raw materials with which the cities and towns and the farmhouses and barns of the Middle West were built.

Lumbering had been carried on in Michigan long before the period of peak activity in the late nineteenth century when it was the foremost lumber-producing state in the country. Small operations, centering around mills such as Adams' Mill, near Plymouth, shown in this painting dated January 18, 1856, supplied the local market in the rapidly developing settlements of southern Michigan.

The lumber industry, as such, however, did not develop until markets opened up outside the local area and outside the state. To take advantage of such markets required large-scale operations, beginning with the land-lookers who sought out the good stands of timber. This sketch of one of these skilled woodsmen accompanied an article in *Scribner's Magazine* in 1893, which was written by the great Saginaw lumberman Arthur Hill, who began his career in the industry in this capacity.

The Landlooker.

166

Courtesy: Mrs. Clover Gougeon

The Bay City lumberman W. D. Young and an employee were dwarfed by some of the pines in one of Young's tracts. Big as they were, however, vast quantities of trees even larger awaited the logger's axe, just as Young himself was but one among many in the Saginaw Valley who made fortunes, large and small, while turning that area into the most important center of the Michigan lumber industry.

Courtesy: Michigan Historical Collections

When the land had been purchased, a logging camp was set up and a camp meant men—men who loved the outdoors and did not object to working from dawn to dusk, six days a week for at least half the year, including the winter months. Such were these men at Reed and Redy's Camp on the Tittabawassee River in the winter of 1890-91 . . .

. . . or these men in a small crew in western Michigan in 1906. Some were only boys while others were much older in appearance than they were in years as hard labor and a hard climate took their toll.

Courtesy: Daniel Thorpe

167

The Kitchen.

Head cook.   Chore-boy.   Cook's "devils."

A good cook was essential to a lumber camp. In a
series of illustrations he did in 1893 for
Scribner's Magazine, Dan Beard made this sketch
of the kitchen in a Michigan lumber camp, with the
head cook, the chore boy, and the cook's "devils."

Courtesy: Grand Rapids Public Museum

The tables in the mess hall are set, ready for the men
to sit down for their meal.

And here was the dinner hour in a Michigan lumber camp,
"drawn from life" by Dan Beard.

The bunk house was home for the Michigan woodsmen from fall
through to the following spring. This was the scene inside
one such bunkhouse, on a Sunday, the only day off the men
got, as sketched by Dan Beard during his tour of several
Michigan camps.

168

Also essential to a successful lumber camp were strong, healthy horses and skilled teamsters who could move the logs out of the woods where they were cut. Some of the teams in the Rust Brothers Camp II in the Saginaw Valley area are shown here in front of the camp's barn.

Courtesy: Michigan Historical Collections

In the woods, choppers and sawyers felled the great giants of the forest, some of which rose to a height of as much as 170 feet and might be three centuries old. A photographer from Chapman Bros. studio in Stanton, in February, 1888, snapped sawyers of the Cutler & Savidge Lumber Company in Montcalm County cutting a felled tree up into lengths to be hauled away by the team which is standing in the background.

Finally, the logs were piled on sleds and hauled out of the woods over the iced roads. There was always a natural interest among the men as to what was the heaviest and tallest load they could haul. A large crowd gathered in the spring of 1892 to inspect this great load, estimated to weigh a hundred thousand pounds, which a team of four horses was bringing to the mill of the Wisconsin Land and Lumber Company in Hermansville.

Courtesy: Manistee County Historical Museum

The famous "big wheels," developed and manufactured by Silas C. Overpack of Manistee in the early 1870's, provided a method of hauling small quantities of logs out of the woods at any time of the year, thereby freeing the logger, to a degree, from the necessity of confining his operations to the months when frozen roads permitted the use of horse-drawn sleighs. . . .

. . . The wheels are shown being used in Oceana County.

Far more important than the "big wheels," however, in opening the way to year-round logging was the logging railroad, first successfully developed by a Michigan lumberman, Winfield Scott Gerrish, in 1877. Scenes such as this one in January, 1882, became a common and welcome sight to the lumberman. Logs are being hauled by horses and oxen out of the forest to this logging train which will then move the load six miles to the Cummer Lumber Company mill in Cadillac. The train is drawn by a tiny Shay Geared Locomotive, which was invented by Ephraim Shay, who came to Michigan after the Civil War and entered the lumber business. His locomotive, which he developed when he encountered difficulty in moving logs to his mill at Cadillac, was manufactured at the Lima Locomotive Works in Lima, Ohio, and was one of the most popular engines used by the logging railroads.

Here in Cadillac in 1882 a narrow-gauge logging train has just brought in a load of 393 logs.

Even after the coming of the railroads, however, the numerous rivers that flow out of the interior of Michigan's peninsulas into the Great Lakes provided the easiest and least expensive means of transporting the logs to Saginaw, Muskegon, and the other great mill and shipping centers. The logs were hauled from the woods to the river bank where they were stacked, awaiting the river drive. These logs at the Clam River banking grounds were the result of fifteen days of hauling over the D. A. Blodgett Logging Railroad in 1884.

With the spring thaw and the breaking up of the ice, the logs were dumped into the river, down a runway, or sometimes down a chute, such as this one on the Big Manistee River in the 1890's, and the river drive, the most exciting aspect of the entire lumber industry, was ready to begin.

It was an awesome sight— the logs filling the length and breadth of the river, with more still to be dumped in from the banks— and this photograph was taken on the Muskegon River in the 1890's, several years after the peak years of production along this river in the 1880's.

Courtesy: Grand Rapids Public Museum

To keep the drive going smoothly required a crew of men trained in the dangerous tasks of spotting trouble spots and moving across the floating logs to prevent or break up log jams. This was part of the crew on the main drive down the Muskegon River in 1886 as the drive passed Evart. In the rear are the floating quarters that were used to house and feed the men.

This picture shows the wanigan or floating cook shack, the cook, his helpers, and some of the river men on the Muskegon River log drive.

Courtesy: Besser Company

Left: The drive ended at the mouth of the river, as here at Alpena, where the logs entered a great "boom" from which they were sorted into pens according to the log marks of the various companies which were stamped in the end of each of their logs. These log marks had to be registered in the county seats of the counties where the companies operated. *Below*: Some of the log marks of companies in the Saginaw Valley lumber area are shown.

Once the logs were sorted, they were fastened together into rafts and hauled to the mills to be cut into timber. These logs at Saginaw, probably in the 1870's, have been pegged and roped together by employees of the Tittabawassee Boom Company, the largest of the companies which handled both the river drives and the tasks of sorting and rafting at the end of the drive.

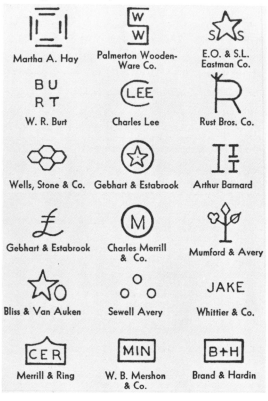

Martha A. Hay	Palmerton Wooden-Ware Co.	E.O. & S.L. Eastman Co.
W. R. Burt	Charles Lee	Rust Bros. Co.
Wells, Stone & Co.	Gebhart & Estabrook	Arthur Barnard
Gebhart & Estabrook	Charles Merrill & Co.	Mumford & Avery
Bliss & Van Auken	Sewell Avery	Whittier & Co.
Merrill & Ring	W. B. Mershon & Co.	Brand & Hardin

Courtesy: Saginaw Museum

Courtesy: Curran Russell Collection

Here was one of the sawmills of the
fabled Louis Sands at Manistee. The
mill is on Manistee Lake at the mouth
of the Manistee River. In the foreground is the Manistee log boom
from which logs are taken to the mill
to be made into lumber of varying kinds
and dimensions which could then be
loaded on board vessels for shipment
out of Manistee.

Courtesy: Clarke Historical Library

Ludington, shown here in 1880 near the peak of the lumbering era in the lower peninsula, was typical of numerous ports along Lake Michigan whose situation could scarcely have been better for the
lumberman. The logs that had floated down the Pere Marquette River arrived at the mouth of the
river which widens into a lake as a result of the natural dam formed by sand bars. Around this lake were
located a number of sawmills and shingle factories. The finished lumber was then loaded on boats at
the docks of these mills, from which point the boats then passed through the channel leading out into
Lake Michigan. (The degree to which the lumber industry attracted foreign immigrants to Michigan
is suggested by the fact that three of the nine churches located on this bird's-eye view were either Ger-
man- or Scandinavian-speaking.)

In the mill towns, the company store sold
a variety of staples, including good old
Log Cabin Maple Syrup, and provided a
place where the workers could gather
around the stove and talk or simply re-
lax, as these men were doing in this un-
identified Michigan company store.

Courtesy: Michigan Historical Collections

Courtesy: Michigan Historical Collections

The boardinghouse was one of the most important institutions in every lumber town. This was Boarding House No. 1 in the Upper Peninsula lumber center of Hermansville in 1891. The place was operated by Mrs. McMonigle and her daughter Rose. They appear at the left. The man wearing an apron was Mr. Fisher, the cook. At the right rear is the home of G. W. Earle, head of the lumber company.

Courtesy: Michigan Historical Collections

The lavish Victorian mansions of the great lumber barons were the most obvious evidences of the enormous profits that many men made in the lumber industry. The home of James Shearer of Bay City, shown here in 1875, was more tasteful than some others because Shearer, in addition to being the successful operator of a sawmill in Bay City, was also an architect.

A half-century later, in 1959, this was the view at exactly the same site, a dirt road following the same curve as the long-since-vanished logging railroad had once followed. The great forest is now only decaying stumps and scrubby second growth.

Courtesy: Michigan Department of Conservation

Courtesy: Michigan Department of Conservation

The story of Michigan's great lumbering days began in the forests, at a scene such as this one in the lower peninsula, in 1905.

174

Courtesy: Michigan Department of Conservation

Between 1901 and 1912, one of the last big virgin pine tracts remaining in the lower peninsula was cut down in operations around Deward, now a ghost lumber town northeast of Grayling, marked by acres of decaying stumps.

Courtesy: Al Barnes

Close behind the loggers came the scourge of fire which swept through the cutover lands, feeding on the cuttings left behind by the lumberman. In the hot summer months, these cuttings became tinder-dry. Any spark might ignite them, destroying in the process thousands of acres of land. This was the scene in the area of the Upper Manistee River after a fire in July, 1894.

The forest fires threatened everything in their path. The great fire of 1871 cut a path of destruction across the central lower peninsula, leaving behind it communities such as Holland, which, as this proclamation of the mayor of the neighboring city of Grand Haven states, was virtually wiped out. By coincidence, this fire occurred at the same time as the great Chicago fire.

The most terrible of Michigan's forest fires was one that roared through the Thumb area in September, 1881, destroying not only much of the remaining timber but vast amounts of farm property as well and killing at least 125 people who were unable to escape ahead of the fast-moving flames. A state marker in a roadside park on highway M-25, near Bay Port, stands amidst some of the forest growth that has come back since 1881.

Courtesy: Michigan Historical Collections

Courtesy: Bay City Times

PROCLAMATION!

Our sister City of Holland is nearly destroyed by fire. More than two thousand people are left homeless and exposed to to the pittiless storm. Food and Clothing is the immediate want.

I, HENRY GRIFFIN, Mayor of the City of Grand Haven, do hereby call upon all good citizens to contribute to the relief of these sufferers.

For this purpose I have caused Subscription Papers to be opened at my office.

Any provisions, cooked or otherwise, and clothing, will be of comfort, and such donations taken to the Office of E. P. FERRY, will be there received and record kept of Donors.

HENRY GRIFFIN, Mayor.
Grand Haven. Oct. 10th, 1871.

GREAT FIRE OF 1881
Small fires were burning in the forests of the Thumb, tinder-dry after a long, hot summer, when a gale swept in from the southwest on Sept. 5, 1881. Fanned into an inferno, the fires raged for three days. A million acres were devastated in Sanilac and Huron counties alone. At least 125 persons died, and thousands more were left destitute. The new American Red Cross won support for its prompt aid to the fire victims. This was the first disaster relief furnished by this great organization.

175

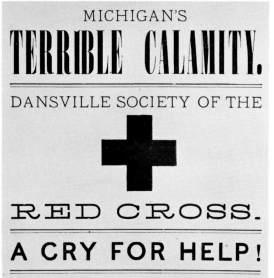

MICHIGAN'S
TERRIBLE CALAMITY.

DANSVILLE SOCIETY OF THE

✚

RED CROSS.

A CRY FOR HELP!

The Dansville Society of the Red Cross, whose duty it is to accumulate funds and material, to provide nurses and assistants if may be, and hold these for use or service in case of war, or other national calamity—has heard the cry for help from Michigan. Senator O. D. Conger wrote on the 9th of September that he had just returned from the burnt region. Bodies of more than 200 persons had already been buried, and more than 1500 families had been burned out of everything. That was in only twenty townships in two counties. He invoked the aid of all our people. The character and extent of the calamity cannot be described in words. The manifold horrors of the fire were multiplied by fearful tornadoes, which cut off retreat in every direction. In some places whole families have been found reduced to an undistinguishable heap of wasted and blackened blocks of flesh, where they fell together overwhelmed by the rushing flames. For the dead, alas! there is nothing but burial. For the thousands who survive, without shelter, without clothing, without food, whose every vestige of a once happy home has been swept away, haply much, everything, can be done. The Society of the Red Cross of Dansville proposes to exercise its functions in this emergency, and to see to it that sympathy, money, clothing, bedding, everything which those entirely destitute can need, shall find its way promptly to them. But the society is in its infancy here. It has in fact barely completed its organization. It has not in possession for immediate use the funds and stores which will in future be accumulated for such emergencies. It calls therefore upon the generous people of Dansville and vicinity to make at once such contributions, money or clothing, as their liberal hearts and the terrible exigency must prompt them to make. Our citizens will be called upon for cash subscriptions, or such subscriptions may be left with James Faulkner, Jr., Treasurer of the Society, at the First National Bank of Dansville. Contributions of Clothing and Bedding may be left at 154 Main street, Maxwell Block, Sewing Machine Agency of Mrs. John Sheppard.

☞A special agent of the Society will be dispatched with the money and goods to see to their proper distribution. Please act promptly.

EXECUTIVE COMMITTEE RED CROSS.

Dansville, Sept. 13, 1881.

DANSVILLE ADVERTISER STEAM PRINT.

Courtesy: Library of Congress

This fire of 1881 in Michigan resulted in the first disaster relief by the newly formed American Red Cross. The relief program was directed by the founder of the Red Cross, Clara Barton, from her headquarters in Dansville, New York. (Estimates of the death toll in this tragedy vary considerably, but the figure of "more than 200" in this handbill is too high.)

Courtesy: Michigan Department of Conservation

Finally, around the turn of the century, the initial steps were taken to conserve what remained of Michigan's once mighty forests. The state and federal forest services began to take action to guard against fires, and at Higgins Lake the state forest nursery began the first planting of seedlings which now have developed into impressive pine plantations.

Monuments often fail to accomplish the purpose for which they were erected, but few who view the Lumbermen's Memorial, placed in a wilderness setting sixteen miles northwest of Tawas City, with the Au Sable River, the scene of so many log drives, just down the hill to the rear of the memorial, can fail to come away without a sense of the tremendous accomplishment of Michigan's lumbermen. Despite their wasteful methods and their lack of regard for the needs of future generations, the results of which can still not be clearly measured, these men, through the more than one hundred sixty billion board feet of pine that they produced, did indeed, as the inscription declares, make "possible the development of the prairie states."

Courtesy: Michigan Tourist Council

The Mining Frontier

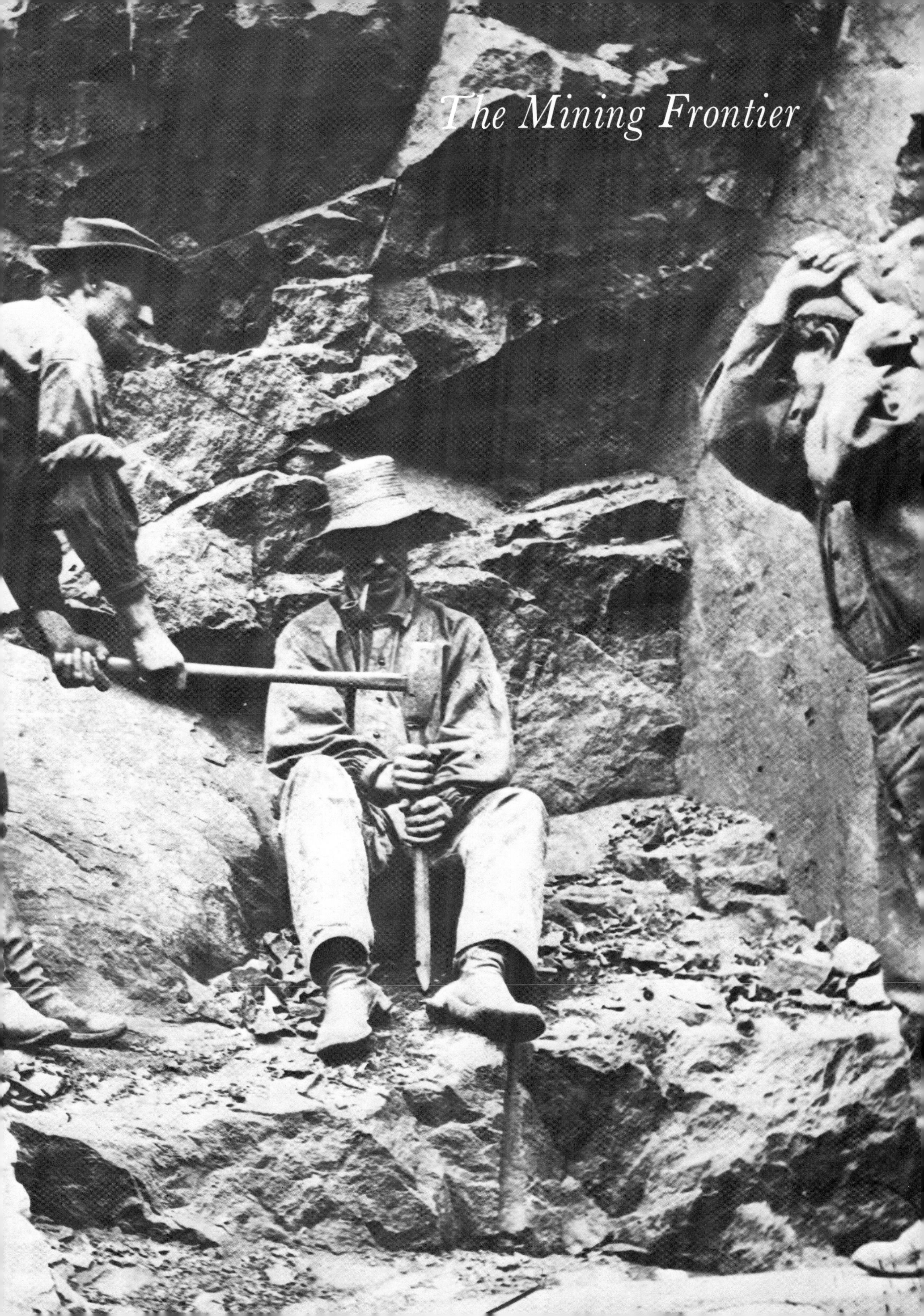

The most famous rock in Michigan history is the Ontonagon boulder, which weighs some six thousand pounds, is fifty inches long, forty-one inches wide, and eighteen inches thick. This is no ordinary boulder, however, as evidenced by the fact that it has been owned and displayed by the Smithsonian Institution in Washington for more than a century. The Ontonagon boulder, which was originally found on the upper reaches of the Ontonagon River in the western part of the Upper Peninsula, contains a huge mass of pure copper, and it was for many years the most visible evidence of the great mineral wealth to be found in this section of Michigan.

Courtesy: Smithsonian Institution

Although upper Michigan's deposits of copper had been known to some of the area's early prehistoric Indians who made artifacts from the outcroppings of the metal in its pure state which they found, the white men who came to the area made almost no attempt for over two centuries to exploit this wealth. In 1841, however, the first detailed scientific report on the extent of these deposits was made by Michigan's first state geologist, Douglass Houghton. The information was contained in Houghton's report on the work of the state geological survey, and despite Houghton's warnings that the mining of this copper would require the expenditure of large amounts of time and money, hundreds of men soon descended upon the Upper Peninsula after a cursory reading of the report, expecting to get rich quickly. The brilliant Houghton, who had already made his mark not only as a geologist but as a chemist and doctor and as a politician (mayor of Detroit), continued the work of the geological survey until his life was cut short at the age of thirty-six when he drowned in 1845 off the shores of the Keweenaw Peninsula, an area that was already becoming known more familiarly as the "Copper Country."

LAKE SUPERIOR NEWS
AND
MINERS' JOURNAL.

VOLUME 1.]   COPPER HARBOR, LAKE SUPERIOR, MICHIGAN, JULY 11, 1846.   [NUMBER 1.

THE LAKE SUPERIOR NEWS,

Is published every Saturday, at Copper Harbor, Houghton County, Michigan, by
E. D. BURR.

TERMS.—Three dollars per annum, invariably in advance.
Advertisements, per square, $1 for the first insertion, and 37 cents for each subsequent insertion.

BROCKWAY HOUSE,
COPPER HARBOR.

THE undersigned would inform the traveling public and those visiting the mineral regions of Lake Superior, that he has erected and comfortably furnished a large and commodious house at Copper Harbor, and is now prepared for the reception and accommodation of guests.

D. D. BROCKWAY.
Copper Harbor, July 3, 1846.

PORTER ISLAND HOUSE,
COPPER HARBOR.

THE subscribers having erected a large and covenient house on Porter's Island for the entertainment of visitors to the Copper Region, would respectfully solicit a share of their patronage.

J. RAYMOND.
H. HAMEL.
Copper Harbor, July 7, 1846.

EAGLE HARBOR HOUSE,
EAGLE HARBOR.

THIS large and commodious house recently erected, and on the most delightful Harbor of Lake Superior, is now open for the reception of boarders and the travelling public.

HIRAM JOY.
Eagle Harbor, July 5, 1846.

VAN ANDEN HOUSE,
SAUT STE. MARIE.

THIS house has been extensively enlarged, newly finished and furnished, and a portion expressly fitted up for the accommodation of Ladies and Families.

J. W. VAN ANDEN.
Saut Ste. Marie, July 1, 1846.

ALGOMAH HOUSE,
SAUT STE. MARIE.

BY JAMES CARSON. The above new and commodious house is now open for the reception of visitors.

JAMES CARSON.
Saut de Stg. Marie, July 1, 1846.

MICHIGAN EXCHANGE,
DETROIT.

D. GOODNOW & SON, successors to Orville B. Dibble, beg to present themselves as proprietors of this extensive and favorite establishment.

Detroit, July 1, 1846.

COMMERCIAL HOTEL,
DETROIT.

JOHN MURRAY has opened the above new and commodious Hotel at the foot of First street on Jefferson avenue, and is now prepared for the reception of travelers.

Detroit, July 1, 1846.

PEAS and BEENS, just received and for sale by
C. R. BRUSH.

Musings by the Lake Shore.

Majestic Lake! Let roll thy troubled waves
Till they recoil upon their mighty source!
A stranger's feet have trod thy shores to-day,
Where many other strangers erst have trod

TWO MONTHS IN THE COPPER REGION.
BY CHARLES WHITTLESEY.

It was on the 14th day of August, 1845, that our party, away on board a staut and well-built yawl, of about four tons, moored in the still water above the rapids of the St. Mary's river. We were venturing upon an experiment.

Courtesy: Sylvester Lucas

By the time of Houghton's death, the Keweenaw Peninsula was in the midst of the first really important mining boom in American history. In an area which as recently as 1842 had been owned by the Indians, towns suddenly appeared, with the early activity concentrated at the northern tip of the peninsula around Copper Harbor, where, in 1846, northern Michigan's first newspaper appeared, its name and the stories it contained obviously reflecting the interests of the area.

179

The expenses involved in establishing a successful copper mine were soon enough to discourage the adventurers and to bankrupt the many companies that were formed in the 1840's. This sketch in the 1850's of the Cliff Mine near Eagle River, the most profitable of the early Michigan copper mines, gives some idea of the increasingly complex nature of the mining operations.

Courtesy: Detroit News

In later years, as the copper deposits at or near the surface were exhausted, underground mining had to be resorted to. Here in 1892 in a candle-lit underground level of a Michigan copper mine, three miners go about their business, one grimly holding a drill which the other two, hopefully, will hit with their sledgehammers, thereby loosening chunks of copper ore.

Courtesy: Michigan Tourist Council

At the surface of the copper mines, a structure was erected over the mine shaft to house the equipment that was needed to transport the men down into the mine and to hoist the ore to the ground level. The most picturesque of these shaft houses was that of the Quincy Mine at Hancock, which was, because of its numerous gables and the interesting lighting effects they created, a favorite of photographers and artists until the building burned in 1956.

To free the copper from the other material found in the ore, the ores had to be crushed and the pure copper removed in a series of operations in stamping and concentrating mills.

Finally, pure copper, concentrated into ingots, was stacked on the dock at Houghton, awaiting shipment.

In the heart of the Copper Country, which stretches from the tip of the Keweenaw Peninsula on the north to the Ontonagon region in the south and west, is Houghton, shown here in 1881, with its twin city of Hancock, a small portion of which shows at the bottom of this view. Located on the waterway which was cut across the peninsula, following the natural water-route system of Portage Lake, Houghton and Hancock became not only major copper-mining centers but also the most important shipping point for much of the copper produced in the entire area.

The great Calumet and Hecla mining operations around Calumet, which began to develop after the Civil War, soon came to dwarf the production of other copper mines and have continued to the present day.

181

Until the late 1880's, Michigan was the leading copper producer in the country. After that, although its production continued to rise for several decades, it lost its national leadership to Western copper-mining states, and ultimately the high cost of mining in Michigan's Copper Country forced most mines out of business, leaving the area dotted with ghost towns, such as Central Mine, located on US-41 in Keweenaw County, where mining ended in the 1890's and the descendants of the Cornish mining families who lived here return each summer for a reunion amidst the crumbling mine buildings and the empty frame houses, once so full of activity and life.

Courtesy: Michigan Department of Conservation

Courtesy: Marquette County Historical Society

Courtesy: Ray A. Brotherton

On September 19, 1844, a surveying team headed by the great William A. Burt, was conducting a combined land and geological survey in the Upper Peninsula on the site of the present city of Negaunee. When the surveyor's compass needle began to fluctuate wildly, Burt called out to his men, "Boys, look around and see what you can find!" In a short time, the cause of the needle's action was found with the discovery of numerous specimens of iron ore. Burt's party had stumbled on the first of the major deposits of iron ore in the Lake Superior region.

The following year, 1845, a group of men from Jackson who had come to the Upper Peninsula in search of copper were led instead by an Indian, Marji-Gesick, to a mountain of iron ore in the area that Burt's party had surveyed. Local tradition in Negaunee declared that the first ore was found amidst the roots of this fallen tree stump.

Courtesy: Victor F. Lemmer

In the next thirty years, the western part of the Upper Peninsula was combed by parties of men, such as this one employed by the St. Mary's Canal Mineral Land Company in 1863, searching for more mineral wealth. Eventually, three great areas of iron ore deposits, known as ranges, were discovered, including the original Marquette Iron Range, which had been discovered by Burt and his men, the Menominee Iron Range, and the Gogebic Iron Range.

Among the most famous of these prospectors was Richard Langford, who came to upper Michigan in the early 1850's. In 1872 or 1873 he claimed to have discovered an ore body which, a few years later, would be exploited by the Colby Mine, the first mine on the Gogebic Iron Range at the extreme western end of Michigan's Upper Peninsula. Langford never received the one-quarter interest in this highly profitable mine that he said he had been promised, and he lived out his life as a hermit, dying blind and penniless at the Ontonagon County infirmary in 1909.

Courtesy: Victor F. Lemmer

This was Peck's Camp, established in 1883 in what would become the mining town of Ironwood. The men in the camp were there to explore for ore, and their efforts ended in the opening of the Pabst Mine, one of the most successful in the history of the Gogebic Range.

Courtesy: Michigan Historical Collections

183

The early iron mines, beginning with the Jackson Mine at Negaunee, the Lake Superior region's first iron mine and for three-quarters of a century one of its most productive and profitable operations, were open-pit mines. This was the No. 1 pit of the Jackson Mine in 1860. The equipment, by later standards, was primitive.

Courtesy: Michigan Department of Conservation

But the bulk of the Upper Peninsula iron ore was found deep in the ground. Here at the Jackson Mine in 1865, horizontal-tunneling operations had begun to reach ore deposits which no longer could be reached conveniently by open-pit methods.

Courtesy: Michigan Historical Collections

At the Aurora Mine in Ironwood in 1886 vertical shafts were beginning to be sunk in order to reach the levels of ore that were located many feet below the surface.

184

This was the famous "C" Shaft of the Norrie Mine at Ironwood in 1899. The mining was now entirely underground, where the ore was loaded into skips which were lifted to the surface by great hoists and then run out along the trestle and dumped, to await subsequent reloading on railroad cars.

To keep the underground mines from filling up with water, like a gigantic well, pumps had to be installed. This is the huge Cornish Pump from the old Chapin Mine at Iron Mountain which was capable of pumping out of the mine three thousand gallons of water per minute.

Mining in the early days was a slow, laborious process, depending on the strength and skill of the individual miners, such as these three workers at the Jackson Mine in June, 1863, pipes clenched between their teeth, who were engaged in the grim business of hand drilling.

A new element of danger was added when underground mining began. These miners working in an Ishpeming mine, depended for light on a candle attached to their hat. If it went out, they might plunge to their death in the darkened underground labyrinth. The miners also faced the constant prospect of being buried alive in a cave-in if the wooden timbers that supported the level in which they were working collapsed; or they might drown if the pump failed and the shaft suddenly filled with water.

185

Iron ore is a bulky product to ship, and thus companies at first made an effort to reduce the ore to pig iron or other forms of iron at furnaces near the mines, using the abundant forests of the area as a source of fuel. One of the most extensive of such operations was at Fayette on the southern shore of the Upper Peninsula, where the Jackson Iron Company built a blast furnace in 1867. It was operated for nearly three decades before being abandoned, a fate all of these forges and furnaces of northern Michigan eventually suffered. The ruins of Fayette today are preserved as a state park.

Most of Michigan's iron ore was shipped out by boat, via the Great Lakes to the iron and steel centers of the East. This was the dock of the Jackson Mine in 1854 at Marquette, a new community on Lake Superior that developed as a shipping port for the Marquette Iron Range.

186

This was Marquette in 1881, by which time the number of mines on the Marquette Iron Range and the total production of ore had vastly increased since the pre-Civil War beginnings. Railroads from the mines to the west brought the iron ore to the docks where it could then be loaded on boats for final shipment to the mills.

This was an early ore train, carrying ore in May, 1865, from the Jackson Mine to the new ore port of Escanaba on Lake Michigan, . . .

187

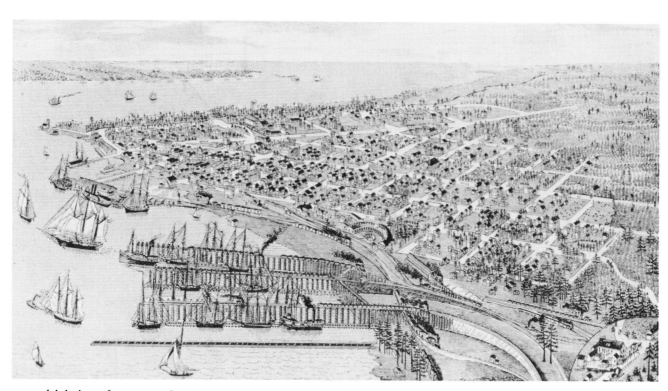

. . . which in a few years developed as a worthy rival of Marquette and later would become the chief outlet for the ores from the mines of the Menominee Iron Range, some thirty to forty miles to the west.

The first small shipments of ore were made in existing vessels, but in 1869, the *R. J. Hackett*, a 211-foot wooden vessel, was built at Cleveland exclusively for the bulk iron ore trade. It became the prototype of the great ore boats that would become the most easily recognized symbol of the Great Lakes shipping industry.

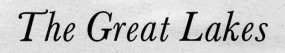

The Great Lakes

CERTIFICATES OF INSPECTORS

In pursuance of the "Act to provide for the

BETTER SECURITY OF THE LIVES OF PASSENGERS

ON BOARD OF VESSELS PROPELLED IN WHOLE OR IN PART BY STEAM,

Approved, July 7th, 1838,"

I, DEWITT C. WHITMAN, having been appointed by the HON. ROSS WILKINS, District Judge of the United States for the District of Michigan, INSPECTOR OF THE BOILERS AND MACHINERY OF STEAM VESSELS for and in the District of Detroit, Michigan, for the time being, DO HEREBY CERTIFY that I have this day EXAMINED AND INSPECTED THOROUGHLY the Boilers and Machinery of the Steam Propeller Independence of St. Mary and that, in my opinion, the said Boilers and Machinery are SOUND AND FIT FOR USE, and that the same have been in use 6 years. Burthen 261 2/95 Tons

In Testimony Whereof, I have hereunto set my hand this 10 day of May A. D. 1849, at St. Mary, in the State of Michigan

Inspector of Boilers and Machinery.

In pursuance of the "Act to provide

FOR THE BETTER SECURITY OF THE LIVES OF PASSENGERS

ON BOARD OF VESSELS PROPELLED IN WHOLE OR IN PART BY STEAM,

Approved, July 7th, 1838,"

I, GEORGE IRVING, having been appointed by the Hon. Ross Wilkins, District Judge of the United States for the District of Michigan, INSPECTOR OF HULLS of Steam Vessels for and in the District of Michigan, for the time being, DO HEREBY CERTIFY that I have this day examined and INSPECTED THOROUGHLY the Hull of the Steam Propeller Independence that said Vessel was built at Chicago in the year 1843, that she has been running five years, and that in my opinion the said Vessel is sound and in all respects sea-worthy, and fit to be used for the transportation of freight and passengers. And, I Further Certify, that she has additional apparatus provided to Steer in case the Pilot or man at the Wheel is driven therefrom by Fire 261 2/95 tons

In Testimony Whereof, I have set my hand this Twenty Fifth day of June A. D. 1849, at Sault Marie, in the State of Michigan.

Inspector of Hulls.

Before the Upper Peninsula's mineral resources could be fully developed and the Great Lakes waterway system completely utilized, the bottleneck of the rapids in the St. Mary's River, where the waters from Lake Superior descend to the lower level of the waters of Lake Huron, had to be broken. Portaging had been the solution since the days of the fur trade, and in 1845 the steamer *Independence* was portaged around the rapids to become the first steamer on Lake Superior. (Certified here in 1849 as "sound and in all respects sea-worthy," the *Independence* blew up in 1853.)

In this 1850 sketch of Water Street in Sault Ste. Marie, the artist Wheaton Metcalf shows how tracks had been laid to make it easier to haul goods around the rapids so that they might be reloaded on ships below—at best, however, a costly method of handling such heavy products as copper and iron.

Then, in the 1850's, the final solution came with the building of the canal around the rapids and the locks needed to raise or lower vessels passing between Lake Superior and Lake Huron, thereby eliminating the need for passengers and cargoes to change vessels. This was the scene as the workers cut through rock to construct the locks.

Many men were involved in the Soo Canal project but Charles T. Harvey, shown here in a portrait made some years later, claimed and probably deserves much of the credit for being one of the prime movers, if not the principal one.

On June 18, 1855, the first ships passed through the locks, the steamer *Illinois* being the first to go up into Lake Superior while the *Baltimore,* shown here, was the first downbound vessel.

191

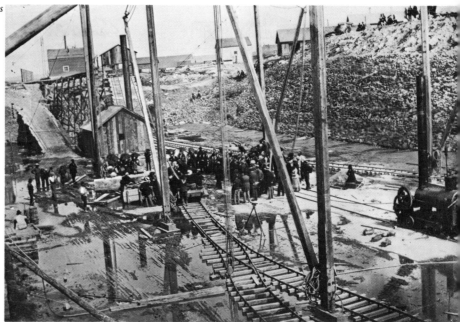

In two decades the total freight tonnage passing through the original locks increased from not quite 15,000 tons in 1855 to more than 1,500,000 tons in 1875. In 1876 the army engineers began constructing the Weitzel Lock, the first of several new locks that had to be built in the years ahead as the canal traffic became the heaviest on any canal in the world. In 1881 control of the locks passed from the state of Michigan to the federal government, since it was felt that Michigan should not have to bear the entire expense of maintaining a facility that benefited the entire nation.

Year-round use of the Great Lakes has always been prevented by the ice which clogs the narrow waterways connecting the lakes, as well as the harbors, and in some cases freezes over the entire lake. Here a small fleet of ships is frozen in for the winter at the Soo in December, 1926, awaiting the spring thaw.

It now became possible to board a steamer in Lake Erie and stay on the same vessel all the way to the western end of Lake Superior, as described here by one of the first steamship lines offering such service.

THE ICE-CRUSHING STEAMER "ST. IGNACE."—Drawn by E. J. Meeker.—[See Page 186]

To keep service operating throughout the winter between St. Ignace and Mackinaw City, the Duluth, South Shore, and Atlantic Railroad developed "an ice-defying ferry boat," as *Harper's Weekly* called it in the story that accompanied this picture layout in 1892. "Yankee ingenuity has circumvented nature in a clever way," the magazine declared, by constructing a vessel that was "like a ram or a steam-hammer, or both combined." In its initial voyage in 1888, the *St. Ignace*, piloted by Captain Lewis R. Boynton, carried a load of eight locomotives across the straits through three feet of ice. The degree to which the eastern end of the Upper Peninsula had been isolated from the world during the long winter months was now substantially reduced.

For many years, however, communications across the frozen waterway that separates Michigan's two peninsulas were maintained by sleds and sleighs pulled by horses or, in this case, by teams of dogs. In the background are the docks used by the ferries that began carrying passengers and railroad cars over the straits in the 1880's.

Another hazard to shipping was the lake storm, such as this one off Sleeping Bear Dune in 1839, depicted in Francis, Comte de Castlenau's *Vues et Souvenirs de l'Amérique du Nord*, published in Paris in 1842.

An artist of the period depicted the sinking of the steam barge *H. C. Akely* in a storm off Saugatuck in November, 1883, traditionally one of the worst months for lake storms. The captain of the *Akely* and five of her crewmen drowned, one of hundreds of such tragedies that have occurred on the Great Lakes since the loss of the *Griffin* in 1679.

As early as 1825 a lighthouse was built by the federal government at Port Huron, and other beacons to aid the navigators of shipping passing through Michigan waters were soon provided at harbor entrances and in dangerous waters. This was a typical Michigan lighthouse of the period, tended by a keeper who, in the automated world of the future, would become as obsolete as the sailing vessel passing by out in the lake.

The Great Lakes were the highways on which a great shipping industry developed in the nineteenth century. Detroit was the chief port of entry into the hinterlands of southern Michigan, a fact dramatically demonstrated in this painting by William J. Bennett in 1837 showing the busy Detroit River and the city of Detroit in the background. The Detroit area was also a center for shipbuilding. The 473-ton, 156-foot steamship *Michigan*, second from the left, was launched at Detroit in 1833 and was the largest steamer on the Great Lakes until it was surpassed in 1838 by the *Illinois*, another Detroit-built ship.

By the time this Detroit waterfront scene was photographed in the last quarter of the nineteenth century, sailing vessels and the early side-wheeling steamships had largely given way to more advanced steam vessels that were capable of carrying much larger quantities of freight and numbers of passengers to and from Detroit's docks.

In nineteenth-century Michigan, however, the waters of the Great Lakes were not only means of transporting goods and people. They were also a source of income for the thriving fishing industry. The fishermen's nets drying on the dock at Whitefish Point in Lake Superior was a common scene along Michigan's more than three thousand miles of Great Lakes shoreline.

This was the commercial fishing fleet at the mouth of the Au Sable River. The waters of Lake Huron outside this harbor were as important to these fishermen and their families as were the waters of the Atlantic to a New England fishing village.

An adventurous photographer went out in a fishing canoe in the rapids of the St. Mary's River and photographed these raging waters where fishing was done with dip-nets and the boats were carried along at a rate of a mile in three minutes.

Courtesy: National Archives

196

Courtesy: Clarke Historical Library

In the winter time on Saginaw Bay, and elsewhere, fishermen went out and obtained great quantities of fresh fish through the ice and brought their catch back on sleds.

The same scene was enacted daily during the fishing season at many other points, such as here at Port Huron in the 1890's, as enormous amounts of whitefish, lake trout, and other fish were shipped fresh or salted to cities throughout the Middle West.

Here at Whitefish Point fish caught in Lake Superior are being brought off the fishing tug and loaded onto cars.

The fishing industry would continue on well into the twentieth century, but it became less and less important and scenes such as this one of an abandoned boat and fish house became all too common—outward signs of changes that were taking place in Michigan.

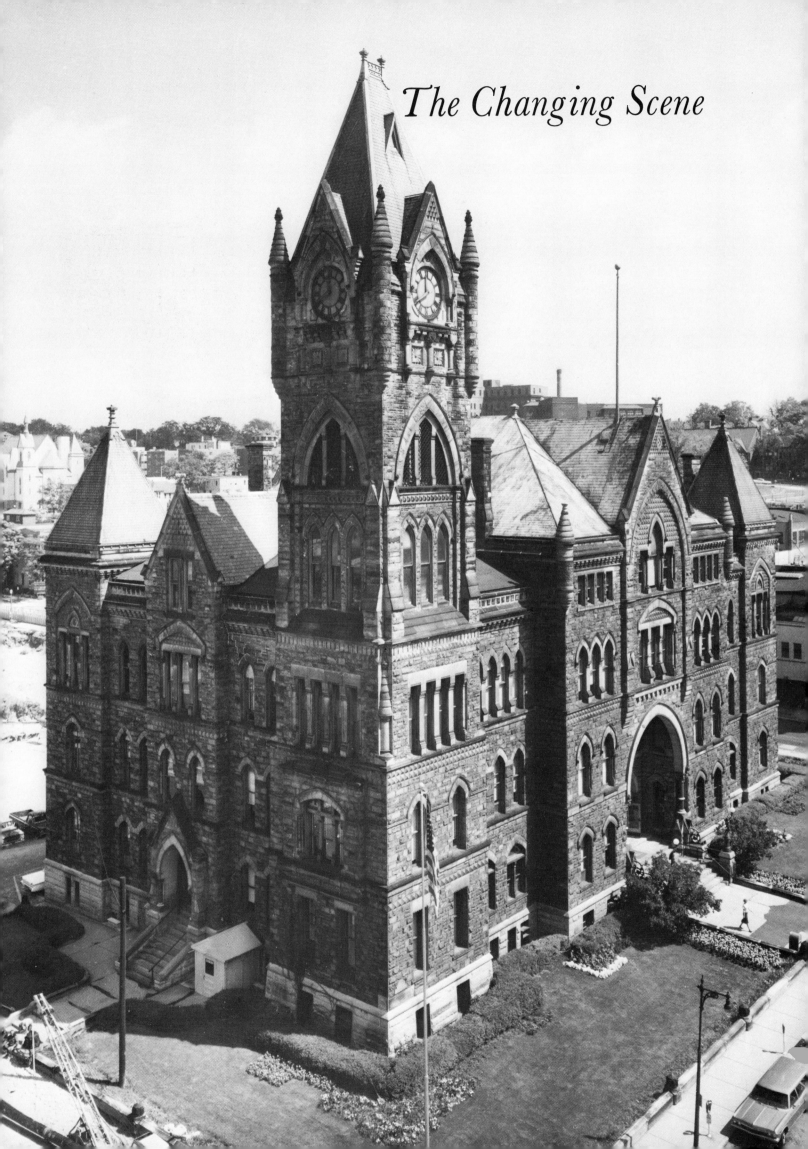

The Changing Scene

Michigan in the latter part of the
nineteenth century was changing rapidly.
It was growing up. In Lansing, in the
1870's, a new state capitol building,
costing over a million dollars, was
erected. When it was completed, its
dome towered over the modest frame
capitol building which a much younger
state had built thirty years before and
which would soon disappear
in a fire in 1882.

Although not as elaborate as some state capitols that were constructed in this period, Michigan's was impressive enough when it opened in 1879 to be the subject of a picture study in *Harper's Weekly*, with line drawings of, among others, the Senate Chamber and the Governor's Room.

Building construction reflected the expansion of the state governmental services in other areas also. At Jackson, in the 1880's, an impressive new state prison was constructed to replace the earlier structures that had been built since Jackson in 1837 was selected as the site of the new state's first prison. By the fourth decade of the twentieth century, however, these new facilities were long since outmoded, and they were abandoned for a huge new structure at a different site. The grim ruins of the old prison remain, resembling some kind of medieval fortress.

At Kalamazoo, where the state's first "asylum for the insane" had been located by legislative act in 1848, this handsome building was erected between 1854 and 1859, according to plans prepared by the Philadelphia architect Samuel Sloan, and Dr. Thomas Kirkbride, of the same city, who collaborated in establishing a new standard for mental hospitals of this period. By the 1960's, Sloan and Kirkbride's work was judged to have outlived its usefulness, and although it was acclaimed by architectural historians such as Harley McKee as "a remarkably advanced building for the 1850's," it was written off by the state as expendable and was scheduled for demolition.

Courtesy: Allen Stross

Courtesy: Allen Stross

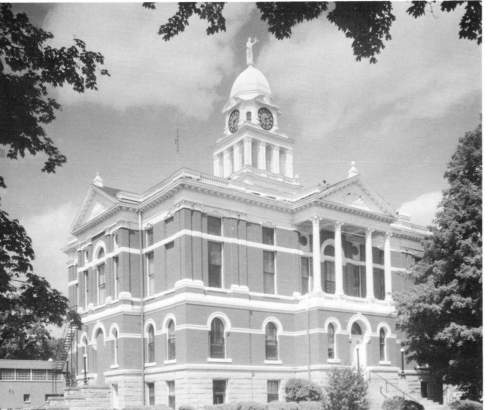

On the county level, the late nineteenth century was an era in which many of the courthouses that still survive and are in use in Michigan were built. A splendid example of the rather eclectic style employed is the Eaton County Courthouse in Charlotte. Built in 1883, it is a red brick building with white trim, topped by a dome on which stands a statue of justice. Eaton County has maintained the building in excellent condition, and when the need for more office space arose the county did a rather remarkable thing: it built new facilities while retaining the old.

Erected in 1888 and demolished in 1967 during America's latest urban renewal craze, **the Grand Rapids City Hall** was designed by Elijah E. Myers, the architect who had earlier designed the state capitol. It was another excellent example of the attention that was given to details, both large and small, in the public buildings of that day which gave to them a distinctive character, details that **many people** of a later, faster-moving generation would regard as fussy an unnecessary.

Education

This was the town of Hillsdale in the 1870's. The houses, some modest, some more pretentious, the fenced yards with the woodshed and privy in the back, the dirt streets—these are what one would expect in a small farming community. But what of the large building in the background? Although it looked out of place, it really was not, because it was part of Hillsdale College, one of many private and public institutions of higher learning founded earlier in the century which now made rapid strides forward that were indicative of the high degree of concern for education that Michiganians shared with the rest of their countrymen.

Michigan, together with the other states of the Middle West, had a heritage of public support for education that went back to the provisions of the Land Ordinance of 1785 and the Northwest Ordinance of 1787. A special, quite unique feature of Michigan's educational development, however, occurred in 1817, only a dozen years after the territory had been established and in a period when the few settled areas were just recovering from the ravages of the War of 1812. The territorial government, under the leadership of Judge Augustus B. Woodward, attempted to set up a complete system of schools from the elementary through the university level, plus libraries, museums, and assorted other institutions— all under centralized control. The entire system was called the University of Michigania or the Catholepistemiad, a name dreamed up by Woodward, who also believed that all disciplines and sciences could be grouped into thirteen categories which he here names and describes. A professor was to be appointed to teach each of these categories in the territory's university.

In the fall of 1817, a two-story brick building was erected on the west side of Bates Street, near Congress, in Detroit. The instruction that was given in this building over the years never advanced beyond the primary and secondary school level to that of a university. Later, the building, the only one erected for the original University of Michigan in Detroit, was used by Detroit for public school classes until 1858 when it was razed.

In 1827, the territory moved from centralized direction of education to complete decentralization, turning over to the townships the power to establish school districts. The first such local district was created in rural Monroe County where the Bridge School District operated from the 1820's to 1955 when it was consolidated into a large school system. The two-room brick school building, five miles east of Dundee, where classes were held from the 1860's, is now owned and preserved by the Monroe County Historical Society.

Through the efforts of the Rev. John D. Pierce (right) and Isaac Crary (left), over-all supervision of Michigan's schools was provided for in the state constitution of 1835 with the establishment of the office of superintendent of public instruction. Pierce was appointed to this office by Governor Mason in 1836.

Courtesy: Michigan Historical Collections

Although free public education was the goal of many educational leaders, it was not until 1842 that tuition-free schooling was provided for the first time in Michigan in this Detroit school, located above a grocery store on Woodbridge Street near Shelby.

In most school districts, until well into the second half of the nineteenth century, tuition was charged. The schedule of fees, according to the course of study the pupil desired to pursue, was set forth by the trustees of the Pontiac Union School in 1851.

208

PONTIAC UNION SCHOOL.

In this Institution, four or five *TEACHERS* are engaged through the year, and all of the Branches pertaining to Primary or Common Schools, are taught. Also, all of the branches usually taught in *Academies*; so that scholars can, in this School, fully prepare themselves for *College*, as well as obtain a thorough education, in the English branches. Scholars residing out of the District, will be admitted on the following

TERMS OF TUITION:

Instruction in the primary department, including reading, spelling, &c.
for a quarter of eleven weeks, - - - - - $1 00
Instruction in Geography, Grammar, Arithmetic, Reading,
Writing, Spelling, &c. - - - - - 1 50
Instructions in same studies as above, including history and
physiology, more advanced classes, - - 2 00
Instruction in Greek, Latin, French, philosophy, chemistry,
botany, Algebra, geometry, trigonometry, surveying,
and higher mathematics, - - - - 2 50
In all cases the tuition of scholars not residing in the District, must be paid in advance, in pursuance of a resolution passed at the Annual School Meeting. No Scholar residing out of the District admitted for less than half a quarter.

TO THE PARENTS AND GUARDIANS OF SCHOLARS

Residing in the District—the District Board would say that they have estimated the current expenses of said School for the ensuing year, at $1,210. To pay which, we have as follows, a tax of $1 00 per scholar.

As per vote of last Annual Meeting, - - $545 00
2 mill tax required by law, to be assessed by the Supervisors, probably - - - 250 00
Interest of primary school fund, - - 166 00
From scholars out of district, (estimated) - 150 00
_____
$1,111 00

Leaving a balance of only $99 to be raised by Rate Bill for the year.

THE WINTER TERM Will commence on the first day of December 1851, and continue eleven weeks, with a school for five days each week. The WINTER TERM will be the commencement of the year.

TEXT BOOKS. Town's Speller, Sanders' Series Readers, Thompson's Arithmetic, Wells' Grammar, Mitchell's Geography, Parker's Philosophy, Davies' Algebra, Davies' Legendre, Andrews' and Stoddard's Latin Grammar, Bullion's Greek Grammar and Reader, Ollendort's French Grammar, Mrs. Willard's Modern Histories, Cutter's Physiology, Comstock's Chemistry, Mrs. Lincoln's Botany.

W. M. THOMPSON. | Trustees. | G. O. WHITTEMORE, *Moderator.*
SAM'L. M. STEELE, | | M. E. CROFOOT, *Director.*
JOHN P. LE ROY, | | JOHN LOCKWOOD, *Assessor.*
HIRAM A. ROOD, |

Dated Pontiac, 14th Oct., 1851. Thompson's Print, Pontiac.

CONTRACT BETWEEN DISTRICT BOARD AND TEACHER.

See Sections 39, 43, 66 and 85, School Law of 1864.

It is Hereby Contracted and Agreed, *Between*

Alfred Gifford of District No. _16_ in the Township of _Flint_, County of _Genesee_, and State of Michigan, and _Hattie E. Southard_, a legally qualified Teacher in said Township, that the said _Hattie E. Southard_ shall teach the Primary School of said District for the term of _Sixteen_ weeks, commencing on the _eighteenth_ day of _November_, A. D. _1867_, and the said _Hattie E. Southard_ agrees faithfully to keep the List and Record required by law, (Section 43,) and to observe and enforce the Rules and Regulations established by the District Board.

The said _Alfred Gifford_, in behalf of said District, agrees to keep the School House in good repair, and to provide the necessary Fuel, and to pay said _Hattie E. Southard_ for the said services as Teacher, to be faithfully and truly rendered and performed, the sum of _Eighty-eight_ —/100 Dollars, the same being the amount of wages above agreed upon to be paid on or before the _first_ day of _June_ 18_68_.

PROVIDED, *That in case said* _____ *shall be dismissed from School, by the District Board, for gross immorality or violation of this Contract, or shall have_ _____ *Certificate annulled by the School Inspectors,* _____ *shall not be entitled to any compensation from and after such annulment or dismissal.*

In Witness Whereof, *We have hereunto subscribed our names this* _eighteenth_ *day of* _November_, *A. D.* 18_67_.

Alfred Gifford .... *Director.*

H. E. Southard .... *Teacher.*

Approved by

_____ *Moderator.*

Crydon Crull *Assessor.*

In this contract with School District 16 of Flint Township in 1867, Hattie Southard agreed to teach the students of the primary school for the sixteen-week winter term at a salary of eighty-eight dollars. She agreed to enforce all rules and regulations established by the board. In turn, Alfred Gifford, school board director, agreed to keep the schoolhouse in repair and provide the fuel to heat it.

In the towns, the first crude school facilities were replaced by larger, more elaborate buildings as the need increased. The architectural style of the Capitol Hill School in Marshall, built in 1860 at 602 Washington Street, reflected the Gothic architectural influence of the period. The building is still used by the Marshall school system, although for storage purposes, not classroom instruction.

The Union School in Niles was typical of the larger, two- or three-story school buildings that were erected in the last half of the century as the city schools expanded to include high school as well as the primary grades.

For the students of Room 3 of the Grandville Avenue School in Grand Rapids, with tiny American flags clutched in their hands, and for their teacher, too, having the class picture taken on the school steps was apparently a solemn occasion. For some of the children, a photographer seems to have been a person who was regarded with suspicion.

But in the last half of the nineteenth century and on into the twentieth, the tiny one-room country schoolhouse remained the most common school building in Michigan.

The University of Michigania which was to have been established in Detroit under the act of 1817 died before it really got started. In 1837, the state legislature provided for a new University of Michigan and located it in Ann Arbor on forty acres of land which the Ann Arbor Land Company had donated free of charge. The company capitalized on the fact that the state university would be established in the town as a means of promoting the sale of a thousand village lots.

This was the interior of the Collins School, a one-room school located three miles east of Reeds Lake. For most of these children, the instruction they received would very likely be all the formal education they would get. Only a few would go on to high school in a neighboring school district and even fewer would go on to college.

The University of Michigan in Ann Arbor developed slowly in its early years. In the 1850's, however, under the leadership of its first president, Henry Philip Tappan, the university began to break out of the traditional classical curriculum and to offer programs in the sciences as well. For example, Tappan decided that the university should have an observatory for classes in astronomy. He raised money in Detroit for such a building, which was opened in 1854, the first observatory in the West and today one of the last structures surviving from this period in the university's history.

Splendid Sale of Real Estate
IN ANN ARBOR,
AT AUCTION!!

THE undersigned will offer at Public Auction on the 8th day of June next, at the Ann Arbor Exchange, in this Village, on the most liberal terms,

1000 VILLAGE LOTS,

comprising some of the most eligible locations for business, and many of the most delightful sites for dwellings in the village or its vicinity. Also,

100 Out Lots

of from 1 to 10 acres each, lying within one mile of the Village; several of them well timbered and many of them well watered, affording excellent pasture. Also a number of

IMPROVED FARMS

situated from one to three miles from town.

The healthy and delightful situation of Ann Arbor and its superior natural advantages are too well known to require description. The Legislature at its last session established the University at Ann Arbor; and also provided by law for the speedy construction by the State of the Detroit and St. Joseph Rail Road, which will probably be completed to this place the present season. The funds of the University being now estimated at over $5,000,000 and rapidly increasing, every thing connected with the institution will doubtless be conducted upon a scale of unparalleled munificence, and nothing will be omitted which science, taste, and wealth can do to embellish the Town, improve the society, and make it the most desirable residence in the Great West, for persons of Literature and refinement, while the great Agricultural, Manufacturing, and Commercial advantages of the place, and the facilities of communication with every part of the Union will afford ample employment for the capitalist and man of business. Similar inducements can never again be offered to purchasers in Michigan.

The terms of sale will be one fourth down, (or approved Bank paper,) and the balance in three equal annual instalments with annual interest secured upon the property.

Ann Arbor Scrip will be received at $200 per share, in payment for all property sold by the Ann Arbor Land Co. ☞The sales will be positive, and the title in all cases warranted good.

E. W. MORGAN, | Trustees of the Ann
WM. S. MAYNARD, | Arbor Land Co,
CHARLES THAYER, | D. B. BROWN,
CHESTER INGALLS, | E. S. COBB,
WM. R. THOMPSON,

Ann Arbor, April 20th, 1837.

ARGUS OFFICE PRINT—ANN ARBOR, MICH.

From 1871 to 1909, James B. Angell was president of the university. These were the golden years when the school achieved recognition as one of the truly great universities in the nation.

The State Street side of the original campus of the University of Michigan in the 1870's looked like this. Many of the trees have grown up with the school and still remain, but the buildings have disappeared.

These are members of the distinguished faculty that had been assembled by the 1870's. President Angell is seated third from the right.

This is a group of the university's students during the same era—sober, well dressed, prepared to face the world.

Medical students tackle some cadavers in their anatomy class in the 1880's. The development of the medical school in the 1840's was one of the clearest indications that the University of Michigan intended to be a full-fledged university.

Important as its academic programs were, another aspect of the university would receive disproportionate attention in the years ahead—years that followed the appearance of the first intercollegiate football team in 1879—the future Champions of the West.

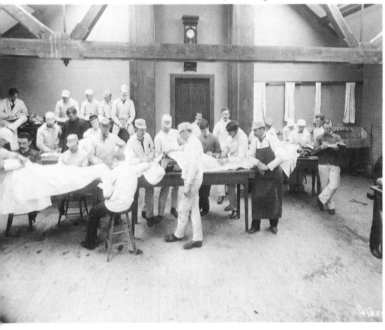

213

Meanwhile, east of Lansing, another state school was becoming well established. After a shaky start following its founding in 1855, Michigan Agricultural College, as this bird's-eye view in the 1879 Ingham County history indicates, had an extensive campus, with the school's farmlands to the rear providing room for the enormous expansion that would be needed in the following century as the school's enrollment went from a modest 264 in 1880 to more than forty thousand by the end of the 1960's.

Courtesy: Michigan State University

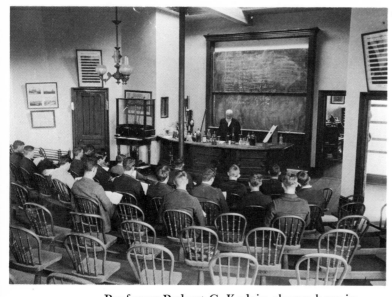

Professor Robert C. Kedzie, shown here in 1892 lecturing to his chemistry class, was one of the most influential Michigan State faculty members in persuading farmers to adopt more scientific agricultural methods and in other ways to improve their economic position. Kedzie and his colleagues thereby built up a backlog of good-will in the rural areas that would prove of inestimable value in securing the school the increased appropriations it would need as it advanced toward ultimate university status.

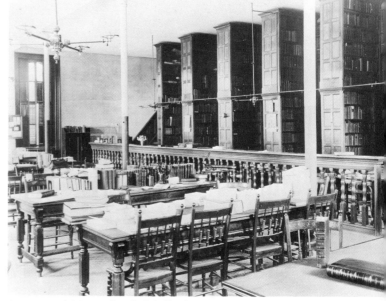

Courtesy: Michigan Historical Collections

At Ypsilanti, Michigan Normal School was established by the legislature in 1849 to fill the need for more teachers. The school's library, shown here in 1894, would need to move into larger quarters twice within the next seventy years as the school's curriculum expanded and its student body greatly increased.

In addition to Michigan's burgeoning system of state-supported colleges and universities, there were scattered through the southern part of the state numerous private, denominational colleges, some of which would die, but most of which survived their initial growing pains. The oldest such college, the Baptist-supported Kalamazoo College, which opened its doors in 1836, began to earn an enviable reputation for excellence under the leadership of its principal, James A. B. Stone, and his wife, the talented educator Lucinda Hinsdale Stone, who headed the college's female department.

214

Courtesy: Burton Historical Collection

Religion and an Urbanized Michigan

Courtesy: Netherlands Museum

This was the campus of Hope College in Holland, Michigan, in 1876. Like almost all the state's private colleges, it was church-affiliated, but its particular affiliation demonstrates the greater diversity in the peoples and their churches that came to comprise the state's population as the nineteenth century wore along.

Hope College was founded by Dutch settlers who had come over from the Netherlands in the late 1840's, under the leadership of the revered church leader Albertus C. Van Raalte.

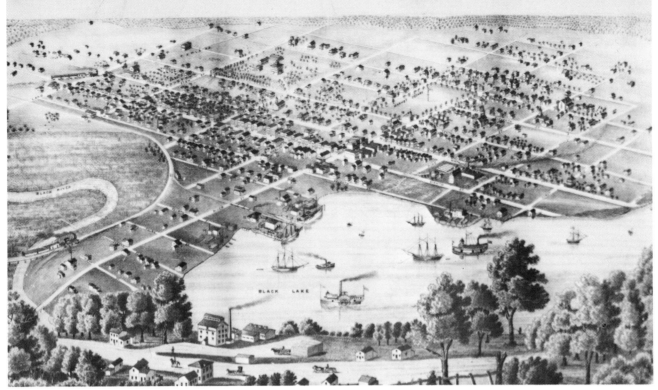

Courtesy: Netherlands Museum

Van Raalte established a colony at the mouth of the Black River, near Lake Michigan, which was called Holland. It is shown here in a bird's-eye view dated 1875, only four years after the community was almost totally destroyed by fire. Holland and its neighboring Dutch settlements in west Michigan added to the state not only a new nationality group but also a new religious denomination, the Reformed Church.

Courtesy: Clarke Historical Library

Germans, virtually unknown in Michigan previously, began immigrating to the state in large numbers in the first half of the nineteenth century. Many settled in the cities where they added an important new dimension to the life of these communities. Typical of this influence was Harmonie Hall, which was built at Lafayette and Beaubien Streets in Detroit in 1874-75, to house the city's oldest musical organization which had been founded by German immigrants in 1849.

Other German immigrants came to Michigan to farm and settled in or near rural communities which almost invariably were oriented around a religious denomination. Most were either Catholic or Lutheran settlements, but in the case of the most unusual of all, the short-lived communitarian settlement of Ora et Labora in the Thumb, shown here in a painting of around 1860, the founders were German Methodists.

217

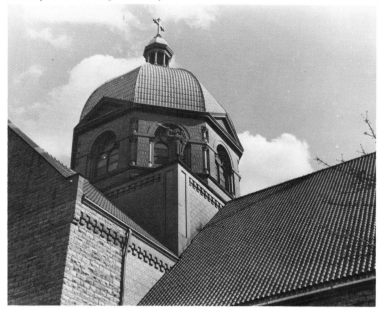

The imposing lines of St. Adalbert's Church, with its archangels blowing golden trumpets, are seen by the modern traveler driving through Grand Rapids on the I-196 expressway. The church typifies the increasingly cosmopolitan nature of Michigan's population in the latter years of the 1800's, for it was built by Polish immigrants who came at this time and became second only to the Dutch in the foreign-born population of Grand Rapids.

The devotion of many of Michigan's European immigrants to the Catholic faith served to strengthen the denomination which had been the only one in Michigan in the seventeenth and eighteenth centuries. In northern Michigan, Father (later Bishop) Frederic Baraga, himself an immigrant from eastern Europe, labored diligently in the middle decades of the nineteenth century among the Indians and the white settlers.

But the astonishing growth that took place in Michigan in a few decades is clearly shown in the character of the church buildings erected during these years. The new St. Ann's Church built between 1818 and 1820 was in itself a considerable advance over the first sanctuaries in which Detroit's original Catholic parish had met in the eighteenth century.

Baraga built many churches, among which the Holy Redeemer Church in Eagle Harbor still stands and is still open for services in the summer months.

218

Courtesy: Historic American Buildings Survey

In the 1840's, Sts. Peter and Paul Cathedral was built at East Jefferson Avenue and St. Antoine's Street in Detroit. The tall spire called for on the original plan was not erected, but in other details the brick church, with its elaborate entrance, was a considerably more imposing edifice than the simple chapels in which Fathers Allouez, Marquette, and the other Catholic pioneers had introduced Christianity to Michigan only a century and a half earlier.

With the influx of Americans into Michigan in the nineteenth century, the Protestant denominations quickly passed the Catholic Church in members and in church buildings. In rural communities of southern Michigan these settlers sought to create the life they had known in the communities from which they had come. In Vermontville's Congregational Church (*above and left*), built in 1843, one could easily imagine that he was in a New England church, rather than in one located in central Michigan.

Courtesy: Allen Stross

The tiny rural sanctuary of the Sashabaw Presbyterian Church in Independence Township, Oakland County, was originally built in 1840 through the joint efforts of the Congregational and Presbyterian denominations, which pooled their resources in the initial missionary work in frontier settlements of the West. Ultimately, the members of these new churches, once they had gotten on their feet, decided with which denomination they wished to affiliate.

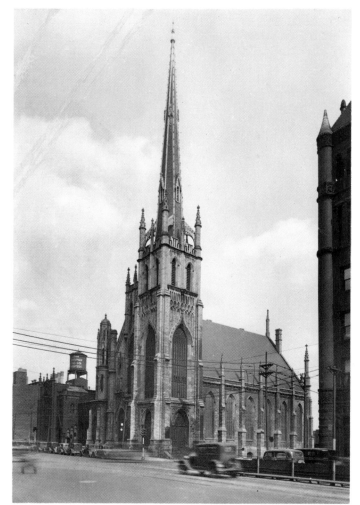

The Fort Street Presbyterian Church at Fort and Third Streets, Detroit, built in 1855, is impressive evidence of the degree to which this denomination was established in Michigan by that date—as well as being an example of the English influence on church architecture of this period. Although it was damaged severely by fire in 1876 and 1914, its appearance today is approximately what it was a century ago.

Similarly, the modest Greek Revival lines of the Dixboro Methodist Episcopal Church, built in 1858, and shown here in an old photograph but still standing today, . . .

. . . were a far cry from those of the First Methodist Episcopal Church of Kalamazoo, erected a few years later.

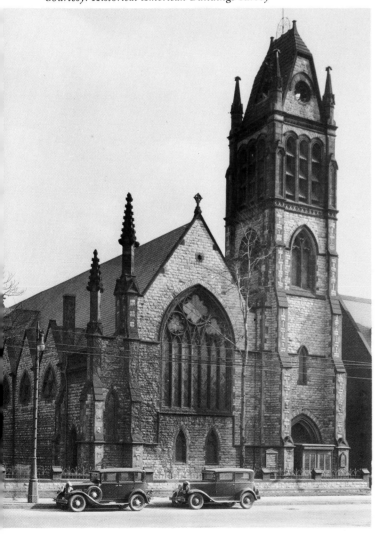

Nevertheless, while a Christ Episcopal Church, at 960 East Jefferson Avenue, Detroit, built in 1861-63, was needed by the large parishes of the cities, tiny church buildings, some of them, such as St. Katherine's Episcopal Chapel near Williamston, built in 1888, of equally distinguished architectural design, were still very much needed in the rural areas.

Some of the most unique personalities in Michigan history represented the smaller denominations. Mrs. Caroline Bartlett Crane, who would become a leading urban reformer of the Progressive era, came to Michigan originally in the 1880's to serve as the minister of Kalamazoo's Unitarian Church.

Courtesy: Detroit News

Courtesy: Stanley L. Johnston

Courtesy: Henry Ford Museum

In mid-century, James J. Strang sought to establish his claim as the chosen successor to Joseph Smith as head of the Mormon Church. Strang founded a Mormon colony on Beaver Island which was achieving considerable success until Strang's assassination in 1856 resulted in the dispersal of his followers. It was Strang's espousal of the doctrine of polygamy and his assumption of the title of king, however, which won him his greatest notoriety with the public, inspiring the unknown artist of the 1850's who painted this highly imaginary scene showing King Strang and his wives indulging in the luxuries of life on Beaver Island.

Then there was Dr. John Harvey Kellogg, a lay member of the Seventh-day Adventist Church, who, as a young boy, had come with his parents to Battle Creek in the 1850's. Within a few years, the Adventists established their headquarters in Battle Creek. Young Kellogg went away to medical school and when he returned to Battle Creek in 1875 he took over the management of the Health Reform Institute which his denomination had established in 1866.

Dr. Kellogg renamed the institute the Battle Creek Sanitarium about the time this photograph was taken in the late 1870's. Here at the "San," which he headed for sixty-seven years, Dr. Kellogg became one of America's best-known medical figures. But it is not for this that he is remembered, important as his medical work was. The name Kellogg became world famous because of the special foods the doctor developed for his patients to make the dietary practices of the Adventist faith as palatable as possible. Dr. Kellogg's investigations proved to be the seed from which sprang a new industry which in turn would help to transform Battle Creek in the years ahead into a manufacturing city.

Courtesy: Burton Historical Collection

Courtesy: Michigan Historical Collections

Courtesy:
Adrian Telegram

Growth—this was the word of the day in the towns and cities of Michigan in the latter years of the nineteenth century. Under the influence of the industrial revolution that was changing the economy of the entire country, some Michigan communities advanced, while others remained stationary. Tecumseh and Battle Creek in mid-century were approximately of equal population. By the 1880's, Battle Creek's population had increased threefold or more, while Tecumseh's had remained about the same. The contrast between the two communities was strikingly revealed in their railroad stations. The Lake Shore Railroad Station in Tecumseh in 1885 was entirely adequate to handle the freight and passenger business of this community which served as a center for a rich farming area. In Battle Creek, on the other hand, a large new depot was built in 1887-88 to handle the increased business of the Michigan Central in that growing city.

Courtesy:
Allen Stros

The contrast between the street scene in Battle Creek in 1860 and that in Jackson only four decades later told a story of improved street paving, larger buildings and many more of them, new transportation facilities—all indicative again of a rapid growth in these urban areas.

Courtesy: Detroit News

Woodward Avenue, Detroit, in the 1890's presented a view that would have been startling enough to Judge Woodward, who had been dead for only seventy years, not to mention La Salle or Cadillac, whose statues looked down from the city hall which had been built in 1870-71. It was no accident that two of the statues on the city hall tower were supposed to represent commerce and industry since these were the forces that were pulling people to Detroit and expanding it from a city with a population of 20,000 in 1850 to a metropolis with one of a quarter of a million by the end of the century. The Majestic Building across the street from the city hall, an early approach to the skyscraper, provided office space for a few of the city's business activities. The tenants entered the building through revolving doors, the first used in Detroit, and they came to work on streetcars. Only one thing is missing—the automobile. Horse-drawn vehicles are still much in evidence, keeping the white-clad street cleaners busily occupied. Within a decade this would change. The automobile would be seen on every street and Detroit, as the center of the most important new industry of modern times, would be leading Michigan into the industrialized and urbanized world of the twentieth century.

226

The Indian community of Middle Village, near Petoskey . . .

. . . the mining and fishing town of Eagle Harbor in the Copper Country, . . .

. . . the farming community of Manchester, . . .

. . . the little boy and his father riding in an ox cart—these were the symbols of an earlier day in Michigan's history, a day that was drawing to a close in the last years of the nineteenth century. The day of the fur trader, the pioneer farmer, the lumberman, the miner, and the fisherman was ended. The day of the factory worker, the white-collar employee, and the scientist was dawning.

Courtesy: Mrs. Otto Lee

228

INDEX

230

232

ACKNOWLEDGMENTS

In selecting illustrative material for this volume, I began with the pictorial collections of the Michigan Historical Commission Archives in Lansing. Although some of the items in these collections were acquired in the earlier years of the Commission's history since its establishment in 1913, it is only in the past decade and a half that a systematic effort has been made to build up these holdings. Under the direction of the present archivist, Dennis Bodem, and his predecessors during this period, Bruce Harding and Philip Mason, and especially through the continuing work during these years of Miss Geneva Kebler and Mrs. Elizabeth Rademacher of the Archives staff, a most extensive file of pictures and maps has been brought together. These have been organized in a logical fashion, greatly facilitating their use.

All illustrations in this book that are not accompanied by a credit line have, in general, been taken from the pictorial collections of the Archives. Many more of the illustrations were also in the Archives but they are credited to the sources from which the Archives originally obtained the picture. Since I also went to many of these same sources and obtained additional pictures which I have credited to these sources, it would be too confusing and not too rewarding to try to provide a complete list of all illustrations, no matter how credited, that have been reproduced from copies I found in the Archives. Suffice it to say that anyone interested in pictures relating to all aspects of Michigan history would be well advised to begin his search at the Michigan Historical Commission.

Important as the collections of the Archives were in my research, more than half of the illustrations in this book have been collected from other sources. It is a pleasure to express my gratitude to the following persons who, either as individuals or as employees of the organization, institution, or business that precedes their name, assisted me in assembling materials and information for this pictorial history.

American Antiquarian Society, Worcester, Massachusetts: Marcus A. McCorison.
Bacon Memorial Public Library, Wyandotte, Michigan: Mrs. Joseph C. DeWindt.
Bartlett, Herbert, Ann Arbor, Michigan, for advice on early maps.
Bay City *Times*: R. Neil Smith.
Burton Historical Collection, Detroit Public Library: James M. Babcock.
Chamber of Commerce of Greater Niles, Niles, Michigan: Justin F. McCarty, Jr.
Chicago Historical Society, Chicago, Illinois: Clement M. Silvestro.
Clarke Historical Library, Central Michigan University, Mount Pleasant, Michigan: John Cumming and Alexander Vittands.
College Sainte-Marie, Montreal, Canada: Paul Desjardins, S.J.
Cunningham, Wilbur M., Benton Harbor, Michigan, who supplied the illustration on page 30 which is credited to its original owner, Cecelia B. Buechner.
Davis, George, Grand Rapids, Michigan.
Dearborn Historical Museum, Dearborn, Michigan: Winfield H. Arneson.
Detroit Bank and Trust Company: Darwin D. Martin, Jr.
Detroit *News*: Ruth Braun and Ray O. Williams.
Field Museum of Natural History, Chicago, Illinois: E. Leland Webber.
Flayderman, N., & Company, New Milford, Connecticut: John Bachner.
Foehl, Harold M., Red Keg Press, Bay City, Michigan, who supplied the illustration used on pages 165 and 167 which is credited to its original owner, Mrs. Clover Gougeon.
Grand Rapids *Press*: David B. Osborne.
Grand Rapids Public Museum: W. D. Frankforter.
Hartford Public Library, Hartford, Michigan: Mrs. J. A. Dohrow.
Haynes, Virgil D., Harbor Springs, Michigan.
Henry Ford Museum, Dearborn, Michigan: John Still.
Kalamazoo *Gazette*: Jean Brink and Robert Maxwell.
Kalamazoo Public Museum: Alexis Praus.

Klima, Joseph, Jr., Detroit, Michigan, who is responsible for most of the photographic reproductions of materials from the Burton Historical Collection which are used in this book.
Lang, Henry C., Fayette, Michigan.
Lemmer, Victor F., Ironwood, Michigan, who, in addition to supplying the illustrations credited to him, also supplied the illustration on page 185 which is credited to the original owner, the Carnegie Library of Ironwood.
Lewis, Ferris E., Henry Ford Community College, Dearborn, Michigan.
Loughin, Mrs. Esther, Michigan State University, East Lansing, Michigan.
Mackinac Island State Park Commission, Lansing, Michigan: Eugene T. Petersen.
Maksymowski, Rt. Rev. Msgr., St. Adalbert's Church, Grand Rapids, Michigan.
Marquette University, Milwaukee, Wisconsin: Raphael N. Hamilton, S. J.
Mason, Philip P., Wayne State University, Detroit, Michigan, who supplied the two illustrations on page 58 which are credited to the original owner, the Buffalo Historical Society.
McCord Museum, McGill University, Montreal, Canada: Mrs. I. M. B. Dobell.
Michigan Department of Conservation, Lansing, Michigan: Russell McKee and Helen Wallin.
Michigan Department of State, Lansing, Michigan: James McClure.
Michigan Historical Collections, University of Michigan, Ann Arbor, Michigan: Robert M. Warner and the members of his staff, particularly Miss Ida Brown and Mrs. Janice Earle.
Michigan Historical Commission, Lansing, Michigan: in addition to those members of the Archives staff listed at the beginning of this section, the following past and present members of the Commission staff contributed in various ways to the success of the project: the former executive secretary, Lewis Beeson, and the present administrative head, Harry Kelsey, and also Donald Chaput, Jack T. Crosby, Jr., John B. Fortier, and Solan Weeks.

Michigan State Highway Department, Lansing, Michigan: Ed Boucher.

Michigan Tourist Council, Lansing, Michigan: William McGraw and John Maters.

Minnesota Historical Society, St. Paul, Minnesota: Eugene D. Becker and Russell Fridley, who, in addition to the illustrations credited to that organization, also supplied the illustration used as background for pages 2 and 3, and on pages 71 and 73, which is credited to the original owner, the Glenbow Foundation of Calgary, Canada.

Monroe County Historical Society, Monroe, Michigan: Mrs. Vincent Barker.

Netherlands Museum, Holland, Michigan: George Cook.

Pilling, Arnold R., Wayne State University, Detroit, Michigan.

Public Archives of Canada, Ottawa, Canada: W. I. Smith.

Quebec Provincial Archives, Quebec, Canada: Bernard Weilbrenner and Antonio Drolet.

Soini, Paul D., Bad Axe, Michigan, who supplied the illustrations on pages 62 and 175 which are credited to the original sources, the Detroit *News* and the Bay City *Times,* respectively.

State Historical Society of Wisconsin, Madison, Wisconsin: Raymond S. Sivesind and Paul Vanderbilt.

Steiner, Fred, Detroit Edison Company, Detroit, Michigan, who supplied, from the files of Detroit Edison, copies of five photographs on pages 143 and 144 which are credited to the original owner, the National Archives.

Stross, Allen, Detroit, Michigan.

Thorpe, Daniel, Wayne, Michigan.

Transportation Library, University of Michigan, Ann Arbor, Michigan: Robert T. Freese and Miss Sharon Hafeman.

University of Michigan General Library, Ann Arbor, Michigan: Mrs. Mary K. De Vries.

University of Michigan Museum of Anthropology, Ann Arbor, Michigan: James E. Fitting.

University of Michigan Photographic Services, Ann Arbor, Michigan: Fred Anderegg and Audie Herndon, who were always patient and prompt in handling the orders for photographic reproductions of so many of the items used in this book.

Wells, Joe E., Michigan Department of Agriculture, Lansing, Michigan.

Western Michigan University, Kalamazoo, Michigan: Willis F. Dunbar and Wayne C. Mann.

William L. Clements Library, University of Michigan, Ann Arbor, Michigan: Howard H. Peckham and Nathan Shipton.

COLOPHON

Plates made by Modern Litho Plate Service, Grand Rapids, Michigan.

Printed by Gilson Press, Grand Rapids, Michigan, using duotone offset process.

Bound by William B. Eerdmans Printing Company, Grand Rapids, Michigan.

Typeface used throughout the book: Baskerville, in various sizes. Captions set in 11 pt. on 13 pt. body on a type area of 42 x 58 picas.

Paper: Warren's Lustro Offset, Enamel Dull, 80 lb. basis, white; by S. D. Warren Paper Company, Boston, Massachusetts.

End papers: Multicolor, ash gray; by Process Materials Corporation, Long Island City, New York.

Cloth: Arrestox Buckram 35350; by Joseph Bancroft & Sons Company, New York and Chicago.

Jacket designed by W. B. Pfaff Associates, Detroit, Michigan; printed by Gilson Press, Grand Rapids, Michigan, using four-color offset process.

Book design and layout by Cornelius Lambregtse.